They Do Remember

Sandy Cicero

Strategic Book Publishing
New York, New York

Strategic Book Publishing
An imprint of AEG Publishing Group
845 Third Avenue, 6th Floor — 6016
New York, NY 10022
http://www.strategicbookpublishing.com

ISBN: 978-1-60693-212-4, 1-60693-212-8
Printed in the United States of America
Book Design: Bruce Salender

Dedication

To my husband,
Jeffrey Robins,
for always seeing the good in me

Acknowledgments

This book does not attempt to explore all facets of society's problems today. It is about one individual who wanted to share her story in the hope of helping others. The story is true, although in most cases the names of individuals have been changed to protect anonymity.

I want to recognize the foster families and other families that gave so generously of their homes and hearts. Words cannot convey my deepest gratitude to the friends and family who helped me through the tough times. I would also like to thank Jeff Robins, Laura Nelson, Jeri Turpin, Charlie Physic, Kathleen Koury, and Shirley Brackett, who gave the priceless gift of their hearts and time. This book exists because of all of you.

Contents

Introduction

MOVING ACROSS THE EARTH IN MANY DIRECTIONS, I looked to find the answers to questions that had haunted me since arrival. Buried deep inside of me was the why am I here. Yet what possible good could come from such a desperate beginning? Also, how am I to reach my final destination?

In the beginning, and for the next thirty years, I was caught in the drama that had been passed on from generation to generation. Questioning all in my path, I received a response: "Stop asking so many questions!"

Not yet having the ability to reach inside, I continued the search on the outside, pondering, wanting to know even the smallest details—maybe to answer the who am I?

Questions that still go unanswered: like "Why Ohio?" Of all the places to be born, I get Cleveland!

Chapter One—Time Travel

LETTING OUT A SIGH, I took my seat on the airplane. As I gazed out the window, the sun's rays washed warmly over my face. The engines roared and the vibrations of the plane rocked me gently into a trance. I was grateful to have a husband who understood and supported me, and relieved he didn't insist on going with me. Seeing my reflection in the window, I took another deep breath. I was not sure why this trip seemed so necessary, but something inside had been nagging me for weeks. Buried deep within my consciousness lay many events and feelings of early childhood. I kept pushing the idea of returning to my hometown out of my mind. It would not go away. I had to go back. I had to go back to the orphanage.

Arriving in Cleveland in 1995 was like entering an old black-and-white Twilight Zone episode. It seemed so dark and dreary. The old neighborhood just looked older. People were not into fixing up or re-modeling their homes. The streets had massive potholes from the severe weather. Old brick buildings stood empty, with broken or no windows. After twenty years of living in the full Technicolor of California, I felt the energy draining from my being as I slowly drove through the narrow streets. The faces were familiar, but I could no longer remember the names.

Following the young girl had become a daily obsession. Attracted to her young, swaying body and schoolgirl innocence, Angelo drove slowly, following alongside of her as she kept walking toward home. Through the open car window he spoke to her, telling her how beautiful she was. He continued stalking her for several days, using flattery until he finally persuaded the blushing girl to get in the car. Amy's resistance wavered. This stranger didn't frighten Amy. She was drawn to the handsome, black-haired, dark-eyed man and flattered that he found her attractive. Pushing aside any thoughts of her mother's warnings, she agreed to get in the car with him.

Angelo Cicero came from a clan of ten. His parents, Biagio and Rosa, came to America from Sicily in 1917. After settling in Cleveland, Biagio went to work for Republic Steel Mill. Shortly afterward he met another immigrant man and was invited to his newfound friend's home for dinner, where he was introduced to Rosa. She was only seventeen and had just arrived from Palermo a few weeks earlier. They were married three months later, and over the next twelve years had ten children.

Angelo, my father, was their fifth child, born in October of 1925. Rosa spoiled him from birth until he was well into his forties. The competition from the other siblings to gain mama's affection only increased Angelo's appetite for more.

After serving in the Second World War, most men returned home more mature; Angelo returned flexing his right fist, making the sailor woman tattoo dance on his forearm. Drinking had become a way of life for Angelo.

Very proud of his Sicilian heritage, he often boasted of wanting to be connected to the mob. His drinking and loose lips kept him from any such ambitions.

What he wanted, he took. Angelo had been a master manipulator and was operating out of darkness. He moved with such ease and strength, attracting young, vulnerable girls wanting to be held in Daddy's arms. Promising the world, he gave only despair. The earth moved for each who received his venom, changing their hopes of deliverance and lives forever.

At twenty-six years old, Angelo showed no remorse when his first marriage ended—after it became known that he had gotten Amy, a fifteen-year-old girl, pregnant. Angelo divorced his wife and did not hesitate to take his first-born son with him. Tony was only four years old.

The Ciceros did not accept Amy into the family with open arms. In their eyes, it was her fault for getting pregnant and breaking up a marriage.

The marriage was condemned from the beginning. Most women in the Cicero family never questioned their husbands—out loud. It was accepted that the husbands cheated on them—and it was considered a relief that they wouldn't be bothered for sex. The women were trained instead to serve their men. Amy had much to learn.

Amy's home life before meeting Angelo had left much to be desired. Her mother, Rebecca, caused quite a stir in her day after marrying her recently deceased husband's nephew. The nephew was twenty years younger than Rebecca. She gave birth to children from both men. Amy—fathered by the second husband—was born in Pennsylvania in 1935. The twenty-year age difference between Amy and her siblings warranted little or no relationship with them.

Her father left for work daily, and when she saw him at night he was drunk and belligerent, or drunk and passed out. Amy's parents fought continuously over his drinking and inability to hold onto a job for any length of time. Amy's mother was a strict disciplinarian, not "sparing the rod" if she felt Amy or any of the others deserved a whipping.

Amy's early life began in a small, musty farmhouse on Delaware Avenue in the backcountry of Washington, Pennsylvania. She left home at an early age and found her way to Cleveland. At fifteen years of age, Amy was working for Dan Dee Potato Chips on the assembly line.

Too ashamed and embarrassed to tell her mother that she was pregnant, and knowing she would get more than a tongue-lashing, Amy married Angelo one afternoon at the office of the local justice of the peace. After marrying, she tried to keep her problems to herself. Her siblings had many of their own concerns.

One of her brothers was into drinking, women, bikes, and guns. He died at an early age.

Another left his wife and children, preferring his own gender.

Her sister, while sleeping, was killed in a fire started by her four-year-old son.

On one occasion, Angelo and Amy had been out drinking with her youngest brother. The three of them decided a visit to Saint Alexis Hospital was a good idea. So just after midnight on New Year's Eve they loudly entered the floor, planning to visit a friend. The event turned into a tragedy when the nurse instructed them to leave the hospital and come back during visiting hours. The trio proceeded to ignore her orders. When the nurse picked up the telephone receiver, Amy threw a fist, punching the nurse in the face. The nurse managed to call for security, and when the guard arrived and attempted to stop the destructiveness of the three unruly visitors he pulled his gun and Amy's brother was shot and killed—taking a bullet aimed at Angelo.

Over the next four years, Amy gave birth to three boys and one girl (me)—all before she turned twenty-one years old.

Birth control was not widely practiced, a fact my mother informed me of more than once saying, "Do you think I would have had all you brats if birth control was available?"

My name is Sandy Cicero. I was born at forty minutes before midnight in April of 1954—a girl, weighing eight pounds eleven ounces. Lucky for me, I had managed to find a copy of my birth certificate.

Mother insists that "my father" forced her to drink. When the two of them drank, violence erupted. I protected myself by hiding under the bed, under the front porch, behind doors: holding my breath. I waited for the fighting to stop, anticipating the worst. My stomach and shoulder muscles tightened as the verbal and physical abuse continued. Protecting myself, I "split off," developing the ability to listen to my surroundings at one level—yet blocking any emotions or feelings at another. I knew enough to stay hidden until the noise stopped. The uncertainty of never knowing what was going to happen next kept me in a constant state of fear. The fighting ended after they ex-

12

hausted each other with verbal and physical abuse—Angelo walking out, and doors slamming.

Mother then moved into her full steam ahead mode, yelling at us to hurry up and get in the car. "I have got to get out of here before your crazy father gets back!"

Grabbing a few belongings, Amy rushed us out of the house and into the car. Racing off to Pennsylvania, we would hide out at her mother's.

The drive from Cleveland to "Little Washington," Pennsylvania was a long and dreadful 135 miles. Amy drove recklessly, mostly along back roads. She made frequent stops. We knew every flashing neon sign along the way invited her into a tavern.

I sat hunched over in the seat next to Mother, as close to a fetal position as possible and yet still sitting. Pulling my knees up under my chin, I kept my head turned toward the window as the tears streamed down my face. I did not want the unwelcome comments from anyone. If my brothers had seen or heard me crying, they would have mimicked and tormented me, calling me a sissy or baby.

If mother caught me crying, her hand whipped around, slapping me across the face, saying, "Now you have something to cry about."

Each tavern stop meant that the three boys and I were to stay and wait in the car while Amy went inside for "a few" drinks. Each stop seemed endless.

While Mother was inside the bar, the boys went wild—poking each other, calling each other names, and making fun of me. But one of us always kept a watchful eye on the door of the bar. Seeing Mother, usually stumbling as she approached the car, we immediately alerted each other to settle down, quickly whispering, "Here she comes." On occasion, Amy even managed to pick up someone to help her with the driving. We dared not question her on who the "someone" was. I found it interesting how many of my "uncles" just happened to be on the way. "Say hello to Uncle . . . " she said as she climbed in the car, seeming not to care that she smelled of booze or that she was filling the air with smoke from a cigarette that dangled from her lips. Her hand gripped several small bags of potato chips and candy bars to feed us. By tossing bags of chips and candy at us, Amy seemed satisfied she had covered the basic food groups.

As we drove on, I tried to sleep. The tainted air and the swaying back and forth of the car sent waves of nausea through me.

Grandma's house sat on top of a hill. I sank lower in my seat as we started up the road and the house came into view.

Mother turned the engine off. No one moved. It looked even worse than I remembered. The house was less than nine hundred square feet, with creaky linoleum floors and a porch, rotting and settling unevenly. Barely visible, the paint was chipped and cracked. Grandma's house had no indoor plumbing.

I waited for the others to stir before I got out of the car, dreading being at Grandma's dreary house once again. Grandma Rebecca heard the car coming up the road and came outside to see who it was. She was standing on the porch with her hands planted on her hips as the car drove up the driveway. In a loud and commanding voice, she barked out, "What the hell did you do this time, Amy?"

Grandma was not one for sympathy or trying to be polite. She rarely used her facial muscles for smiling. I cringed at the sight of her. Rebecca's dress was old and faded, hanging loosely on her oversized body with a stained apron tied around her bulging waist. She was not your cuddly, sweet-smelling grandma. I found her body odor of sweat and snuff disgusting. Seeing Grandma bend over and spit into one of the many tin cans placed beside the furniture in the house was not a pleasant sight.

I was annoyed by their double messages. Spitting for the grown-ups seemed to be okay, but not for the boys. Questioning either Grandma or Mother led to the same reply, "Don't do as I do. Do as I say!" Or the short version of the same response: "Because I said so!"

Questions concerning mother on anything, including family heritage, usually brought a backlash of comments, avoiding real answers. At times, she claimed to be a hillbilly, Pennsylvania Dutch, and Irish and, still other times, Indian. Amy did remark on occasion that it was her Indian blood that allowed her to drink so much. But more often the answer had always been, "Why? You writing a book?"

I detested having to sleep with Grandma. Once, I looked over at her while she lay sleeping, her lips parted slightly as the brown slime dripped from the corners of her mouth—a tobacco chewing woman all the way.

Amy usually left us with her mother while she went into town on the pretense of looking for work.

With no indoor plumbing, Grandma gave us our baths in a large, round tin pan down in the basement. A "girls first" rule applied. The boys sat watching, hiding at the top of the stairs and making faces at me. The only thing I detested more was having to empty my bladder in a pot located in the closet. Expressions like "they didn't have a pot to pee in" confused me. Was having one supposed to be a good thing?

Sandy's father came to the rescue

Father generally arrived a few days to a week later. Retrieving us, Angelo then drove us back to Cleveland—Amy not included. Once back in Cleveland, he would disperse us among his side of the family. Angelo seemed to make a game out of "let's hide the children," clueless as to what this was doing to us. He plotted ways to keep Amy looking for us. This seemed to bring some sort of perverse pleasure for him and angered Amy.

The news of Rebecca's death in December sent us on our last mad dash to Pennsylvania. Rumor had it that Rebecca had died with a telephone in one hand and a bottle in the other. "Your grandmother was a god-fearing Jehovah woman. She never touched a drop of alcohol except for medicinal purposes," Amy later disputed in her harsh, snapping manner. *Sandy's grandma died*

When we arrived, instead of grieving relatives I witnessed people ransacking the house looking for possessions or money. The not-so-grieving relatives searched until evening, under mattresses, behind picture frames, in the basement—everywhere. Each hoped to pocket anything of value. Mind boggling—one look at the house told me there was nothing worth looking for. No one else seemed to pay any attention to Grandpa, who sat quietly rocking in his chair, drinking one of several beers to follow. The house later became property of the state, because no one could afford to pay the three hundred dollars in back taxes.

The funeral was later that night. Family members passed in front of the casket to view Rebecca and commented, "Oh, look how good she looks. I've never seen her look better!" Was this a compliment?

searching for... *the gma by* *"relatives" took advantage of*

Grandpa William was so intoxicated that he had to be escorted from the funeral parlor. In his attempt to lean on the casket for support, he had to be stopped before tipping it over. Everyone gasped. I was starry-eyed and confused.

The "scavengers" gathered later for a drink at the bar setup located in the basement of the funeral parlor. One aunt, with a glass in one hand, had the nerve to pull on the arm of her child and whispered loudly enough for me to hear, "You stay away from those Cicero children. They're all rotten, the whole bunch of them!"

Years later, while reviewing a copy of grandma's death certificate, I found another piece of the puzzle. Grandma Rebecca was born in 1889, in Monongahela, Pennsylvania. Had it not been for the name of a nearest relative being listed —one whom I had never heard of—I would never have known of yet another sister Amy had. I've yet to get a straight answer from Mother about her nationality, much less why she failed to mention she had another sister.

Chapter Two—Hide and Seek

ANGELO DROPPED ONE BOY off at each of his brothers' houses, leaving me with his parents. He knew my mother was terrified of his father Biagio, and she would not come to get me while there. Grandma Cicero, Rosa, always greeted me warmly with a smile. She also never forgot birthdays. Even with thirty-five grandchildren, each received a dollar if one happened to visit her on or around a birthday.

Rosa was nineteen years old when her first child was born and thirty-nine with the last. She was a full-time homemaker. Rosa stood five feet tall and had a wonderful childlike laugh. I took great pleasure in the sound of her broken English, even though this meant struggling to understand her. Looking back, Grandma was the only family member who showed affection toward me, holding hands as we walked together to the neighborhood corner market.

I was five years old and followed Rosa from room to room like a small puppy. The fear that I had become accustomed to when with my parents ceased when I was with Grandma. I enjoyed being with her as she went through her daily routines. She braided and twisted strands of her long, graying hair into a bun each morning. Preparing meals from scratch, she pounded and rolled out dough for pasta or bread. With Grandma, I could relax and just be a kid. She was thoughtful and loving, making sure I had something to do—such as the coloring books she bought for me. I sat for hours, coloring in the books while she made dinner. I took pride in coloring and waited for her praise.

Grandpa (Da's Side)

Biagio worked long hours, and when not working he enjoyed his wine cellar, growing vegetables, and playing the accordion. He was not a man of many words—yet, when he did speak I, like others, trembled in fear and sensed the threat behind the words: "I'm a goin a tella you, onea more time—little girls are not supposed to . . . !" Father later spoke of Biagio's abusive behavior when he was growing up, and told us how lucky we were not to be getting a beating by Grandpa with his razor strap.

Sundays meant spaghetti dinners and relatives coming over. Grandma cooked, while Grandpa's idea of spending time with me meant sitting silently together outside on a wooden bench, swatting flies. I was anxious to see my aunts, uncles, and cousins, and waited for them to arrive. But after they arrived, I was hurt that they spoke mostly in Italian around the house when they didn't want me, the other children, or guests to understand what was being said. The family members didn't want us to know what they really felt about me or my parents. I sensed their pity or scorn as they discussed us.

Of the ten children that Biagio and Rosa had together, Angelo was the one who gave them the most obvious trouble. Angelo was the first to divorce, and to do time in the state mental hospitals and the penitentiary.

I was told many times what a problem Father was. Relatives would say behind his back, "Your damned father."

And yet they always made small talk with him when he was there.

②

Grandma was the only one who kept silent about Angelo. I'm unsure of how long I stayed with them or why I was moved once again.

Next, I was moved to Uncle Guido and Aunt Edith's. No one bothered to explain why. I sat in the kitchen chair, wondering how long I would be staying.

Aunt Edith raced up and down the stairs to the basement, moving with great speed as she put the meals together. I wondered where she was going and why she had to move so fast. The house was kept immaculate. All chores were done by a self-induced, strict schedule.

Family – cousins/aunts – not able to coming

Then, moved to Uncle Guido + Aunt Edith's house

Each day was planned from morning till night. Aunt Edith stayed busy all the time—cooking, cleaning, and running up and down the stairs to the basement. Expecting help from no one, she received none.

Uncle Guido was obtrusive, loud, and mean spirited. He not only screamed at his wife and their children, but he made remarks about every program and actor he watched on TV, and every passing stranger on the street was judged harshly. Guido didn't have to be upset about anything. He just yelled for the sake of making sure he was heard. "Hey, Edith, get me something to drink!"

He demanded that everything be done by his command at once. Everyone was on guard, waiting for the attack when Guido was home. If there was any affection for one another in this household, I certainly never felt it. But they did have spaghetti every Sunday and the unspoken rule was that all the family members were expected to show up for dinner.

And I learned something else from living with them; I resented being a female. While the males sat in front of the TV watching their favorite sports event, the women ran around the kitchen preparing their meals and waiting on them hand and foot. The guys joked about the perfect woman being blind, deaf, and mute.

When I wasn't in the kitchen helping, I kept busy outside. My cousin, Alfredo, and I were close in age, and he was the only one I really remember at that time. He had two older brothers and a sister, but they didn't hang around the house much. I think the oldest brother had gone into the service. His sister was old enough to be dating a guy who lived down the street a few houses away. His other brother could fill volumes on his own.

Anyway, Alfredo and I used to sneak out of the yard whenever the opportunity presented itself. The neighbors behind the house had a swing—an old tire that hung by a rope from a tree. One day while playing on it, I lost my balance and fell to the ground, bouncing my head on the ground hard enough to cause double vision along with a painful headache. It was impossible for me to hide my problems from my aunt. After coming home, I stumbled a few times and spilled milk trying to fill glasses for dinner. She and Guido drove me to the emergency room. I was treated and released, but had to sit in the car and listen to Uncle Guido carry on about how he told us to "stay in your own damn backyard."

Aunt Edith called me in one day and instructed me to wash up and change my clothes. She seemed nervous and made no eye contact when she told me, "Your father is coming to see you."

My parents and the Cicero family have the annoying habit when speaking to me or anyone about other family members—not using names when addressing someone. It is always "your father," "your mother," "you kids." This somehow made it "your fault."

I do not know how long it had been since I had last seen Father. I was impatient, excited, and scared to be seeing him. Somehow, even through all the fighting and moving us around over the years, I still managed to think Father was the good guy. Angelo was certainly more fun at times to be with than mother; he often took me to the barbershop, telling me what a "big girl" I was, and letting me get my hair cut in the barber chair—then telling me how nice I looked with my new haircut. Only his real goal for the boy cut was to anger Mother. She wanted the only girl to have long hair. Mother was never pleased when I came bouncing through the door, beaming, "Look at me." I was always hurt, knowing she hated me when she snapped back, "You two think you're so damn funny!"

I sat in the kitchen chair, close to the door—waiting and watching for Angelo's car to pull in the driveway. The 1960 Chevy came to a stop at the bottom of the stairs that led up to the kitchen. Leaping from the chair, "He's here!" I yelled out as I raced through the door. Father was not alone in the car. My brothers, Albert, Mario, and Sam grinned at me from the back seat. Angelo nodded, "Hello. Get in the car. I'm taking you guys out for ice cream."

Climbing inside the car, I sat next to Angelo in the front seat.

Chapter Three—Penguins

AFTER DRIVING LESS THAN TWENTY MINUTES, and still anticipating the ice cream, we drove up a long, unfamiliar, winding road. At first, I thought we were in some sort of park. There were huge manicured green lawns on both sides of the road, surrounded by tall trees far off in the background. Randomly placed around the lawns were several life-sized statues. There was a white statue of a woman with her head bowed and hands held together in prayer, a long-haired man with his arms around two small children, and others. I questioned Angelo, "What is this place?" No response.

We drove in silence. The car rolled to a stop in front of a red brick building or cottage. No one spoke as Angelo left the car. Looking away from us, he told us to "Stay put. I'll be right back." Not moving, our eyes followed his steps as we watched him walk up the sidewalk leading to the doors of the cottage. He disappeared from sight. Sensing something was not right, even the boys remained quiet.

When the doors reopened, walking a few steps behind Angelo was a lean, tall woman who was dressed very peculiarly. She wore a long, black gown with what looked to be white cardboard around her neck and forehead, showing only a portion of her face and hands. Mario broke the silence and spoke up in the back seat, "Hey, look at the penguin!"

Mario's humor didn't work this time. The two approached the car. I felt only the lump rising in my throat; I was frozen and unable to speak.

Angelo stopped walking to light a cigarette, letting the nun walk ahead of him. Opening the car door, she spoke with authority. "My name is Sister . . . Please come with me children."

I looked to Father. "Go on. I'll come visit you as soon as I can," he said. I protested, "COME VISIT! Why do we have to go with her? Who is she? Where are we?" I questioned strongly.

Again in a commanding tone, "Come along children," Sister repeated as she took hold of my hand and led me away from the car. I stubbornly resisted her pulling on my arm. Before any of us could realize what was happening, the car with Angelo in it drove away. Albert, Mario, and Sam huddled closely together, staring at the ground as they followed behind us. I kept looking back, trying to see what was going on. Where did my father go?

Entering the dimly lit cottage, I felt a cold shiver. Fear mounted inside of me. The footsteps that approached across the hard wooden floors jolted me back to attention. The nun forced a frown on her stern face, as we were greeted by yet another nun and a priest. At seven years old, I was introduced, along with three of my four brothers, to the Catholic orphanage, church, and school system.

I was told to go with Sister Mary Beth—that she would take me to my cottage. Trembling and silent, I followed her to Cottage Thirteen, my new home for the next three years. My brothers followed the priest to the boys' cottages on the opposite side of the grounds from where the girls stayed. They lived there for five years.

Parmadale was built in the early 1900s on close to two hundred acres. In addition to being an orphanage, the facility was used by the Cleveland court system to house children while custody or other family problems were being disputed. Like Disneyland, people came from all over the world to see the attractions. But it felt more like the local animal shelter. The children were viewed like puppies: "Oh, look at that one."

I saw little of my brothers over the years. The only thing that made me look forward to attending church in the mornings was the opportunity to see them from across the room.

Sister Mary Beth did not like anyone to turn around during church services. Unfortunately, she sat directly behind me, watching closely when I did try to turn for a glimpse of my brothers; she placed her hand firmly on my head and forced me to look forward. Sister Mary Beth had no patience for disobedience. "You will follow the rules around here, young lady, or I will have to send you to a place for children who haven't yet learned to behave properly."

I felt no love, compassion, or understanding while in Parmadale. Individuality and questioning on any subject were not tolerated. No one bothered to explain why we were now living in an orphanage. Each morning I woke hopeful someone would come and get us out. Mother or Father had never waited this long before coming to get us. Each night I moved about restlessly in bed feeling disappointed, scared, and alone. Why did they not want me? Why did they not want the boys? We were not bad.

The militant nuns kept the order. They followed their routines by the clock, morning till night. Clapping of hands started or ended each event.

I followed the girls around with uncertainty, managing to get through the day until it was time to get ready for bed. On my first night in Parmadale, I jumped as Sister Mary Beth clapped her hands and barked out commands to me and the other girls in the cottage. Once upstairs in the large impersonal bath area, we were ordered to remove our clothes down to the white cotton slips. I sat stubbornly staring at the floor. I wasn't about to get undressed in front of all of them. And besides, I didn't own a white cotton slip.

Sister Mary Beth snapped at me. "You will get undressed now or you will find yourself standing outside the back door for the night."

She must be joking, I thought. She was not. I was marched down the stairs with her fingers digging into my shoulder, as she led the way and put me outside the back door. I fought back the tears, not wanting her to see me cry. But once the door slammed shut, I burst into tears. Within moments, defiance struck me as I bolted down the stairs and began running. "I am not staying here," I told myself as I continued to run into the nearby woods.

I had never been outside alone at night. It was muggy and hot as I ran through the dark woods. The moonlight was hidden by the thickness of trees.

I stopped running and began moving very cautiously. The night shadows frightened me. The light summer breeze moved the leaves on the trees. Crackling noise from my own footsteps caused my heart to pound harder. I stopped crying. The path was getting darker in front of me. Fear held me motionless. Afraid of the darkness and not knowing what was ahead of me, I was forced to turn back, walking quickly back toward the cottage. Trying to catch my breath, I stopped at the bottom of the stairs before I slowly climbed up to the door.

Standing outside the back door, pounding my small fist against the steel door, I pleaded, "Let me in."

"Let me in," I repeated.

Sister Mary Beth finally came to the door and stopped only to peer at me through the small glass panel. Before opening the door she questioned me, "Are you ready to do as you're told?"

I nodded in agreement.

"I can't hear you!"

"Yes," I said, defeated.

"Yes, what?" she demanded. "Yes, Sister," I answered, looking down at my feet as she finally opened the door and I stepped inside. The heavy door slammed shut behind me, and with the closing of the door I closed the door to my heart, forcing myself to submit, and followed the nun upstairs.

Sister Mary Beth stood, patrolling each of us with her watchful eyes. The other girls had not yet showered. I was instructed to hurry up and get undressed and join the girls as they stepped into the one shower area. There was no privacy and it was very unnerving for me. The voices and laughter of my brothers came back to me: "Look, she's naked."

There were ten fixtures on each side of the long, narrow room and enough room in the middle for the nun to pace. We lined up in front of a showerhead. With the only set of on-and-off controls at the entrance to the shower stall, the nun controlled the water flow. She left the water on just long enough to wet our bodies. With the clapping of the hands and a voice command, we began to wash. Before we were allowed to rinse, the nun walked through the shower stall and made sure we had each completely covered our naked bodies with soap.

Once satisfied, she returned to the controls and turned the water on briefly for us to quickly rinse. I loathed taking showers with all the other girls. It was humiliating, parading butt-naked in front of the others.

So many Brothers

The days were tedious. We had to learn all the many rules and time schedules, and what was demanded of us. Even though my home environment had been so unstructured and unpredictable, I was at least able to escape and be alone with my own thoughts. The nuns, with their rules and schedules, didn't allow us to be children. This was unbearable for me. Going to bed at night, even with all the others in the dorm, I felt so alone. I was a light sleeper and any sound in the dark would wake me. Often, it would be muffled sounds of one of the other girls crying. Wake-up calls always seemed to come early.

With the sharp clapping noise of her hands, the nun stood in the doorway and spouted loudly, "Prayer time, girls."

The clapping stopped only long enough for her to flash the lights on and off, on and off, on and on. The rumbling sound began as twenty girls hurried out of their beds to recite the Morning Prayer. I didn't bother to sit or stand—I just rolled out of my bed and slid to the floor, falling into a kneeling position. Following our morning prayers, we put on slippers, made our beds, and stood at the foot of the bed. It was only after inspection of all our beds that the nun released us to proceed into the bathroom area for more ritual.

We each removed toothbrushes from our bathroom lockers and stood in front of the long, white sink that was equipped with ten faucets on each side. The nun came around to put the toothpaste on our brushes. Only after each girl had her toothpaste would she then give the command, "Okay, brush."

I grudgingly hurried about each task, not wanting to be the last one done. The mockery from the other girls and, worse yet, the sharp tongue of the nun would surely follow.

Each day blended into another. Regardless of the day of the week, the routine was always the same: wake up, make your bed, shower, get dressed. We were expected to go to chapel in the morning, then breakfast, and then school. The only exception was that we didn't go to school on weekends.

Even changing your shoes became a never-ending chore. We were to wear slippers upstairs. Before going downstairs, we had to change into tennis shoes to walk around in the cottage. And before going outdoors we changed into one of three pairs of black-and-white saddle shoes—one pair for school, one for church, and one for any of the other activities. These shoes had to be cleaned and polished once a week.

Twin beds lined the walls on both sides of the room. Each was spaced about four feet apart and covered with a green army blanket. Each child was assigned a number that identified our locker, clothing, and personal belongings. Not only was I living in Cottage Thirteen, but now I was assigned number thirteen.

The nuns were programmed for strong discipline and punishment, "for the good of the child."

We anticipated impending doom when the nun entered the room and positioned herself in front of the lockers. Sitting in a chair, she instructed everyone to line up. She sat, glaring, and called out the number of the child who was to move forward and receive punishment and ridicule. Whether it was your turn to be punished, or someone else's, the pain was felt by all.

When one of us did not move forward quickly enough when called, she would nod her head toward a few of her "trained pet" girls, instructing them to grab hold of whoever was to be reprimanded. When "13" was called I went kicking, screaming, twisting, and turning, trying to fight off the girls as they dragged me and held me over the Sister's lap with my pants down. She proceeded to spank my bare bottom with the rubber sole of a tennis shoe. I cried or rocked myself to sleep most nights that first year.

The cafeteria-style food brought me many anxious moments. I hated the cooked cereal—especially oatmeal. The smell alone sent waves of nausea through me; I cringed at the sight of the thick, lumpy, pasty blob being shaken from the wooden spoon into my bowl. As soon as I returned to my seat at the table, I looked around the room, anxiously hoping the nun was not watching me. The moment the opportunity presented itself, I managed to switch bowls with Heather, the girl who sat next to me each day. She seemed to enjoy eating everything and anything, gladly accepting a second portion.

One morning, however, I was unable to make the switch. The nun was standing guard close to my table. As each girl finished eating, she had to stand behind her chair and wait for all the others to finish. I sat with my head down, stirring the now cold blob before me, pretending not to notice the sound of the Sister's shoes tapping impatiently on the floor. Finally, tired of waiting, the nun stood me up in front of everyone and proceeded to spoon-feed me. I was so humiliated. Not wanting to look at all the eyes upon me, I stared down at the floor, listening to the sound of the spoon scraping the plastic bowl. Sister Mary Beth made sure to pull the spoon upwards each time and clean it off across the tips of my upper teeth. As she smugly scraped the last spoonful into my mouth, she questioned me. "That wasn't so bad, was it?"

With that, I threw up all over the front of her starched, white bib collar.

The chapel and school were in one building, located about two hundred yards from the cafeteria. Between cottages and to the other buildings, we seemed to spend our days going back and forth, up and down the flights of stairs and in and out of our lockers—always putting on a different pair of shoes.

We filed into the chapel each morning and took our assigned seats in the pews. The lineup was from the smallest children in the front pews to the tallest in the back. I sat and knelt next to the same girl every day. Cecile was the only child smaller than me.

This girl had a very annoying habit. As soon as she would go into a kneeling position, she began to make a disgusting noise—sucking the fluids that dripped from her nose back inside her head and wiping the rest into her "praying hands." Still pretending to pray, Cecile slid one hand at a time down her sleeve or dress to dry them, as though no one could see her. But I did. Week after week this went on.

I put up with this—until one day! On this particular morning, I just couldn't control the anger that was building up inside of me. I was already sick to my stomach from the scent of incense as the priest waved his arms around the room, filling the chapel with the distasteful odor as he chanted in Latin. Just as I did not understand or speak Italian, I didn't know Latin either. And my knees were reddened from kneeling. Suddenly, I got right in her face and began to mimic her disgusting noises and gestures by wiping my nose up and down my arms.

I totally lost control and was unconscious of my surroundings until I was whacked on the back of my head. The nun had approached me from behind. She grabbed me by my hair and dragged me out the side door, slamming me up against the brick building. I was frustrated because she would not listen to my explanation, and she proceeded to slap me across the face for questioning her about singling me out for punishment. Winded by the whole episode, and my cheek stinging, I refused to cry as she scolded me about my behavior in the house of the Lord.

Schooling was another area of structure and discipline—sit up straight, put both feet on the floor, no talking, and pick up your pencil only after being instructed to do so. At times, the only sound in the room would be that of fabric rustling between the nun's legs as she walked, and the clicking of beads from the rosary hanging around her waist. I sat there, dreading the nun as she crept up and down the rows of desks in her soft-soled, black shoes. She carried a wood ruler in one hand and tapped it against her other. "Okay, pick up your pencils and begin!" she barked.

My mind started spinning: I hate tests. Who cares if I don't pass? She can't make me! Upset, I just sat there. The nun moved closer to me. "I said begin, Sandy." Picking up my pencil slowly . . . begin what, I thought. Tell her I can't remember anything. Sitting still and just holding my pencil, I waited for a moment of inspiration. The Sister's voice came snapping at me, "Stand up, young lady!"

When I stubbornly refused to hold my hand out, she grabbed my wrist and used the ruler on the back of my hand, hitting me across the knuckles.

Another time, I called a girl a liar and was punished after being overheard by the nun. The nun's fingers dug into my shoulder as she marched me to the corner of the room and proceeded to stuff a bar of green, Lava soap into my mouth. I was left to stay in the corner for two hours while the other girls came by to make fun of me. She informed me that additional time would be added on for each time I attempted to remove the soap. The following morning my lips were blistered and cracked.

The nuns found different methods of punishment, all in the name of God: "He will get you if you don't be good."

To me, this meant the nuns would get you. I was locked in a small, dirt dugout in the basement, left kneeling for long periods of time, scrubbed floors with toothbrushes, and was slapped, spanked, and had my hair pulled on more occasions than I care to remember.

On Saturday nights, we sat and watched television—Lawrence Welk, the nuns' favorite show—while our numbers were called to have our finger- and toenails trimmed by the nuns.

Sunday was visiting day. This meant getting dressed in our Sunday best, polished black-and-white saddle shoes, and clothing that was donated by different charities. I waited and waited in front of the television set—not watching the TV, but the sidewalk outside—hoping the next set of footsteps would be that of my own parents. Anticipating the sounds of approaching footsteps, each time my body stiffened, and then I sighed with disappointment at the sight of someone else's parents.

I was always jealous of my brothers. At least they saw each other on a daily basis.

Amy and Angelo found more excuses for not coming to see us. They left us waiting for their appearance more often than not. During the next three years, they managed to visit us separately or together only about once a month—some months not at all. This was not because of a distance problem. I realized, years later, that Parmadale was located only about ten or fifteen miles from where my parents lived. The boys managed to escape on several occasions and jumped on a bus for the ride into Cleveland—only to have Mother return them within the hour.

In April of 1962, my father, mother, and Uncle Guido showed up together for Parmadale's presentation of "Holy Communion." The photos paint a picture of a perfect Catholic family. Mother was dressed in a knee-length wool coat with fur trim around the collar. Both men were dressed in suits and ties. Each visit left me confused, lonely, and scared. How could my parents come only to visit us? Why did they leave us there? Would they come back again? I was eight years old. This was the last time I was to see my parents together.

There were practices that, today, still seem truly bizarre even for the nuns to request—like dictating the time of day we went to the toilet. They marched us in and had us sit on the toilet until we produced a bowel movement. And we weren't able to flush the toilet until the nun inspected it and nodded for us to flush.

At other times, without explanation, we were given a small, round box and instructed to place our bowel movements in it. God only knows what this was for——maybe they received charitable donations in return for our deposits!

One evening, we returned to the cottage after dark and someone had left the back door open. When the lights were turned on, those of us standing in the front of the line screamed as we were greeted by the flapping wings of a bat, flying from wall to wall, looking for a way to escape.

Sister Mary Beth induced even greater fear in all of us as she ordered us to wrap our heads in a towel, warning us to hurry. "That bat will get tangled up in your hair!"

Even after the nun closed the dorm door, I spent that summer night with my head buried under a wool blanket, sweating and hiding from the creature that roamed about, trapped like we were. The maintenance man arrived in the morning and succeeded in freeing the bat.

Winter months proved trying as well. We marched over to the clinic each morning and waited in a single-file line for a turn being spoon-fed a tablespoon of cod liver oil. I cringed and usually gagged before being able to hold my breath and swallow the greasy syrup. I watched a few of the girls being able to hold it in their mouth long enough to get outside and spit it out without being caught.

We had very little unstructured play time. I usually drifted off, preferring to spend my time in solitude. Alone, I was content. Comforting myself by sitting and rocking gently back and forth, I talked to my "imaginary friends." Staring down at the linoleum on the floor, each spot in the pattern became a friend—one who would listen. I told my friends of all the mean-spirited things the nuns, and sometimes the older girls, did. I told them of how one day I would escape this awful place. While other children played, I sat motionless—until instructed by someone in authority to "stop your daydreaming and go be with the others!"

I heard somewhere that if you pulled a dandelion carefully from the ground, did not disturb the ball of whispery feathers, and blew on it—causing all the seeds to fly into the air while making a wish—that your wish would come true. I wanted to believe in something, so I spent many of my days picking dandelions and blowing the heads off the feathery fluff. To me, these were not weeds: they were the flowers of hope that would help me to escape.

I only got to speak to my brothers on visiting days. I looked forward to seeing them. Mario made a joke out of just about anything and could make me laugh when he bragged about the many things he did. One of his favorites was singing the music from a Nancy Sinatra song. Only he changed the words to, "These witches are made for flying and that's just what they'll do. One of these days, these witches are gonna make stew out of you." He claimed that if you wanted to rattle a nun, you should start singing that tune.

About once a month, the evening routine was broken when we were treated to a movie in the auditorium. The orphanage filled our heads with propaganda from every Hollywood film ever produced that showed how lucky we were to be in a Catholic orphanage. I waited for the nuns at Parmadale to show the same kindness displayed on the screen. I waited for Bing Crosby to appear, but he didn't.

The message was always the same—good girls become nuns. I had no desire to place my whole body face down on the aisle of a church, professing my love to a God that all shared and to whom all nuns were married.

The Catholic system drummed into me, "Don't question authority—your parents or any adult. Honor thy father and mother."

I could not quiet the voices inside my head that questioned what "honor" meant—especially for the authority figures I had known until now.

I mostly sat daydreaming in church, sometimes wondering why God let his only son get hung on a cross. I worried that if we were all God's children, what was going to happen to us?

School classes were interrupted one day as a nun entered our room and announced that the President of the United States had been shot. We were instructed to leave the classroom at once and follow her to the chapel. After spending several hours in the chapel that day, we were kept sitting silently in front of the black-and-white TV for three days watching the funeral. This was the only time the nuns showed their emotional side. During those three days, I saw in passing a few nuns returning teary-eyed from morning chapel. What was the big deal?, I thought, people die every day.

Each child or family was assigned a social worker by the county. Ours, Mrs. Foyer, came out to see us occasionally. The only use her visits served was to allow me to visit with my brothers for a short while. She usually dropped the four of us off in some room while she stepped out.

I do remember two visits in particular. One visit was to inform us that my father had "hurt" my mother—that she had been hospitalized. "Your father has been sent away because of the serious nature of his actions."

During the other visit, I was given two options—to stay in Parmadale or go into a foster home. I had been in the orphanage for three years now, and the prospect of living there forever was terrifying to me. Albert tried to talk me out of going into foster care. He thought we should all try to stay together. I contended that any place would be an improvement to staying in Parmadale. And I didn't feel as if we were "all together" anyway. I was isolated on the opposite side of the grounds, housed with the girls.

It wasn't long before I was placed in my first foster home. I was ten years old.

Chapter Four—Home Is Where I Lay My Head

MS. FOYER TOOK ME TO INTERVIEW with the Conway family once, before having me placed in the home. The Conways had a modest, new ranch-style home in the suburbs.

The day had finally arrived. The social worker made small talk with me as we drove to the foster home. I was terrified. The only place I wanted to be going was home—home with my own family.

Judy sat next to me on the white-on-white floral sofa and smiled often as she explained the family's situation. Her husband, Jack, wanted to be there to greet me that day, but his work schedule would not permit it. Their son, Joey, was with his grandparents and anxious to meet his "new sister." He would be home shortly and the baby, Tammy, was napping. "We can go in and check on her a little later."

I sat wide-eyed, hands clasped together on my lap, trying to be polite and cute. I knew this was what grownups liked.

Judy walked Ms. Foyer to the door and assured her, "I know we won't have any problems with Sandy."

As the door closed, Judy turned back in my direction and pointed to the small suitcase I arrived with. "Honey, you can bring that with you and I'll show you your room."

The room was decorated brightly, in sharp contrast to the dreary dorms and dark green army blankets I had left behind in Parmadale. A white bedspread with yellow and pink flowers covered the twin bed. I was stunned and excited to learn I would have the room all to myself.

Judy opened a dresser drawer and helped me unpack the box. "I can't believe this is all you own. This certainly won't do. I will have to get you more clothes for school," she replied.

Judy was twenty-seven, very attractive, and fashioned herself after the popular former first lady, Jackie. She wore her hair stacked up in a French twist and carried herself with elegance even when dressed in a pullover sweater and cotton shorts. She was a real talker. In addition, when she talked, whether on the telephone with her mother or while visiting with Mrs. Vanesky from across the street, Judy had a cigarette and a coffee cup in her hands.

Jack Conway was not home much. He was tall and impressive in his navy blue work uniform. He adored Judy, had a gentle manner of speaking, and a sarcastic sense of humor I found most amusing. Jack worked swing shifts for an airline and was not home or awake during the day. His time off work was spent out in the garage, fixing one of the cars; or he was in the basement, developing hobby photos in his darkroom.

Joey, my foster brother, was four years old and seemingly happy. He had all the comforts of a nice home. When not sleeping, he was running wild and playing with no concern for where he would be sleeping each night.

Tammy was a year old when I came to live with them. She had a beautiful face, wavy blonde hair, and shining blue eyes. I sensed Judy's sadness as she tried to explain to me why Tammy could not get out of bed—that she was born with cerebral palsy.

The excitement of being out of the orphanage began to diminish. Once again, I was faced with learning a whole new way of life. The Conways tried to make me feel welcome and at home, but I never felt as if I fit in or belonged. This was not my home. These were not my parents. I wanted to scream when I was introduced as Mrs. Conway's daughter, "What is wrong with you people? Stop staring at me. Yeah, you figured it out. You can see she's not my mother." She had blonde hair and blue eyes, and mine were brown.

Judy was very demanding, always expecting me to look and behave in a certain way. On school nights I had to curl my straight hair, struggling to sleep through the night with hard plastic rollers pressing into my head. Each morning, I dressed for school in one of the store-bought dresses that Judy had picked out. I wanted only to blend into my new surroundings. I was accustomed to either hand-me-down clothes from my brothers or the clothing from Parmadale. Instead, I stood out in my bright, colorful, frilly dresses with ribbons tied in my now overly curly hairdo.

School was difficult for me. It seemed the harder I tried to pay attention the more I split off. It was not unusual for me to find I had turned several pages in the assigned text, stopping at some point, realizing I hadn't retained a single word.

Judy tried working with me each night. We sat at the kitchen table. She drilled me endlessly—going over and over the material. I sat in fear, knowing one wrong answer would lead to the backlash of insensitive comments. "Oh, come on Sandy. You know the answer! Now, what is the matter with you?"

Even knowing the material that night, I knew it would be lost to me the next day. As soon as I heard "Okay, pick up your pencil and begin," I split off.

I was envious of Joey. He knew how to play, how to have fun, and he knew how to get what he wanted. If he was watching television and an advertisement came on for some new toy, Joey would shout, "I want that."

If Judy said, "We'll see," or "No," Joey's response was always, "That's okay. Grandpa will buy it for me," as he marched toward the telephone. Calls to Grandpa reporting the item he wanted seemed frequent.

Joey did what he could to get attention in the home. Cries to his mother that I didn't do something he demanded, or that I hit him, happened all too often. It never occurred to me that Joey might have been just as confused about my being there as I was, and possibly he did not like the idea of another kid coming into his home and taking his parents' attention away from him.

I grudgingly prepared Joey's breakfast on the mornings that Judy slept in. I waited for him to make a decision on which of the numer-

Joey — step brother

ous boxes of cereal he wanted. "You pick it out," he cried. Yet the game was the same each morning—I knew he would not like the one I picked out.

Judy step mom

One morning, as I was pouring the milk on his cereal, I heard Tammy choking. I put the milk jar down on the table, raced to her room, and held her until the convulsions stopped. Meanwhile, the milk jar slammed to the floor in the kitchen, shattering the glass and waking Judy from her sleep. Joey reported to her that I threw it on the floor and, one more time, succeeded in getting me blamed for something I didn't do.

I tried so hard to please Judy, wanting her to love and accept me. I never felt good enough. I helped with taking care of Tammy and Joey, and I helped with the cleaning and ironing—lapping up any bit of praise. It wasn't until years later that I realized how much the family did enjoy having me live with them, even if I was difficult at times. Joey expressed to me how much he enjoyed having an older sister to play with.

stepsister, Tammy had cerebral palsy

Tammy's smiles touched my heart. I cherished holding and rocking her, wanting only to be near her. For the first time in my life, I felt needed and loved. Now, I had someone in my life I could hold and talk to. Opening myself to her gave me much joy and happiness, not understanding that her illness was as critical as it was. Tammy, unable to develop normally, needed to be watched all of the time. The cerebral palsy kept her from learning to do the things a child her age would do naturally. She never learned to sit up, crawl, or walk. Her frequent episodes of convulsions were frightening to experience, for her and the family. At times, I would hear her choking noises and I would run to her room just down the hall from mine. Grabbing hold of her, I would put one hand behind her neck. With the other, I reached for a tongue depressor to place in her mouth to prevent her from swallowing her tongue. I would hold her until the convulsions stopped, praying that God wouldn't let her die. Other times, Judy or Jack would get to her first. I lay in bed, afraid to move until I knew she was all right again.

Jack and Judy had a few parties in the basement entertainment area, which was complete with a bar. Now ten years old, I helped with the cleanup—helping myself to as many sips of alcohol that were left in the glasses by the guests as possible. I wanted to be a grownup. I mimicked what the adults were doing. Even though I didn't like the burning sensation of the liquor as it went down my throat, I did enjoy the warm feeling it gave me shortly after swallowing it.

Lastname of step parents

I had lived with the Conways for almost a year; Tammy was suffering with convulsions more and more frequently. The day came when it was necessary for her to be hospitalized. I hurried home from school every day, hoping Tammy had returned. I missed her so much. The house seemed so empty with her away. I found myself waking at night, going to her room only to find her bed empty.

Tammy died in October of 1965. Seeing her small body lying still in the casket was unbearable. I wanted to reach down and pick her up, to hold her as I had for the past year. Why did God take her? The pain cut through me. I wanted her to open her eyes. I wanted to be able to make her smile. She brought comfort and joy into my life. Her smile had helped me through so many tough times. I was furious at God for taking her life, and not mine. She had family who loved and needed her. I couldn't understand why God didn't take me. But I did hear the message in life, "Only the good die young." *— step dad*

I was grief-stricken and too young to know how Judy, Jack, and Joey were dealing with Tammy's death. I only remember that Judy had closed off Tammy's bedroom. No one was to enter. Everything was to be left untouched. I couldn't understand what was happening. But the day came soon afterward when Ms. Foyer arrived. I was taken to another foster home. I do not remember saying good-bye or leaving that day. I only knew that Tammy was gone, and I never said good-bye to her. *social worker*

Catherine Giaimo had heard of me from her sister who had taken in foster children from Parmadale. Her sister had recently taken in one of my brothers. After his speeches about foster homes, I was quite annoyed to discover that Albert had agreed to go into one.

Catherine's sister told her that Albert had a little sister in Parmadale. When the Giaimos inquired about me they learned I had already been placed in a foster home. Within two weeks of Tammy's

2nd Foster Home *[handwritten annotation]*

death, they were contacted by Ms. Foyer, who informed them that I was ready to be placed in their home.

The Giaimos lived an unpretentious, traditional life with loving family values. They were sensitive to each other's needs and the family came first. Ben and Catherine had two daughters (Lucy and Marge) who were living at home, and two daughters (Will and Jo) who were married and out on their own. *4 daughters [handwritten annotation]*

They treated me as if I were one of their own daughters. For the first time since leaving Grandma Cicero's, I felt accepted at least most of the time. But they had their hands full. They were neither told of the circumstances that brought me to Parmadale, nor the reasons for leaving my first foster home.

I offered no explanation of my own and little more upon questioning. Withdrawing more and more from life at the age of eleven, I did not let anyone get close to me and mostly kept to myself. I only participated when I was asked to.

Mrs. Giaimo was patient, kind, and tolerant of my many moods. She tried her best to make me feel welcome and a part of the family. She spent many occasions sitting across the kitchen table from me, arms folded in front of her and her eyes and voice pleading with me to talk to her. "'What is wrong, Sandy? What can we do to make you happier here?"

The truth was I didn't know. I didn't think about being happy—I liked them. I liked being around them. Catherine was a wonderful cook and, as did Grandma Cicero, she took great pride in her home and cooking.

I lived moment to moment, waiting for the news that they couldn't handle me anymore and were sending me back. I waited for the social worker to show up and move me elsewhere. I waited for my parents to come and get me. I wanted to go home. I couldn't accept the fact that I didn't have a home to go to—that my parents weren't coming.

Catherine and Ben never insisted I call them Mom and Dad. Nevertheless, I did at some point.

Ben was warm and funny. He was a short Italian with a dark tan. When not working hard in construction, he played hard in his garden. Each spring, he plowed up more and more of the backyard, making room for a bigger garden. Unlike most of the folks in the neighbor-

Welcoming Family [handwritten annotation, left margin]

hood who had pink flamingo lawn ornaments, Ben proudly displayed a white statue of the Virgin Mary in the center of his garden. Ben cherished his family and spent most of his free time with them. On occasion, he did invite the guys over for poker.

He was always ready to help me with my homework or school projects. I remember the science project he helped me to create. It was a cotton plantation built upon a large piece of plywood. I was so proud to take this to school.

My foster sisters, Lucille and Margaret Ann, were great friends to me and accepted me into their home. I often wondered how they felt about having another girl brought into their home. They all fascinated me. They were open, loving, and funny.

For the first time in my life, I saw a family that communicated with one another and enjoyed their time together. They all participated and expressed themselves, sometimes loudly, but never seemed to take one another for granted. I could see and hear the kindness expressed between them.

I grew closer to the family than I wanted to. It was difficult to remain aloof when they were all dependable and followed through on what was said. Life with them was less painful. I tried not to think much about the day I would move on.

School friend

Shirley Brackett and I met at school. She lived down the street from the Giaimos' house. Her parents had divorced, and she now lived alone with her father. Shirley's father worked late, giving us time alone after school to drink from his bar. Afraid of what might happen to us if her father found out we had been into his liquor, I assured her he would never notice if we added water to the bottles.

My moods and personality changed after I had only a few drinks. Returning from Shirley's after school to the Giaimos, I was in a foul mood. But the words only ran through my head. The words were lost inside of me, my face fixed with a look of defiance. I spent a lot of time in my room, trying to escape through sleeping or reading.

Catherine had fought with Ms. Foyer on several occasions, trying to convince her that they needed more money to provide me with adequate clothes for school. The few things I had arrived in weren't going to get me through the school year. I didn't like seeing her going through so much trouble because of me. I had also kept quiet about, yet wondered, what had happened to all the clothes I left at the Conways.

Ben injured his back on the job and he was forced into taking an early retirement. Now, the family had to manage on a fixed income. But they seemed to always pull together and managed to get through the rough times.

The holidays were filled with family, kids, food, and lots of laughter and fun. We lived in the basement most of the time. It was set up with a complete kitchen and living room. The upstairs was only for sleeping or company other than family. We also went upstairs to sing together in front of the hi-fi stereo, singing along with Mitch Miller, Perry Como, and Frank Sinatra. One of these guys even had a bouncing ball to help us follow along with the words on the TV.

Ben and Catherine were beaming with excitement on the day the new stereo arrived. The girls went wild with joy as they watched the console being carried into the living room. Hugs and screams of excitement filled the room. Lucille was the loudest.

I continued to test the emotional stability, patience, and good nature of the family. No matter how bizarre my behavior was at times, they were always there for me. I had never had this kind of acceptance or love, and I was afraid of it.

It was September and only two weeks into a new school year. I was now entering seventh grade. On Monday morning, I sat in homeroom and listened to the principal over the intercom system. The class sat restlessly while the principal's voice bellowed out the day's events. He ended with, "Sandy Cicero, please come to the principal's office following this morning's announcements." I left school and walked home after someone in the principal's office informed me Mrs. Giaimo had called, requesting that I return home at once.

I had a sinking feeling that the outcome was not going to be pleasant. Was it something I had done? Could it be something was wrong with Catherine, Ben, or the girls? I wanted to run, but I couldn't. I was in no hurry to find out what was in store for me, and took my time as I walked back to the house.

My heart began to beat faster. I looked up the street toward the house. Recognizing the red convertible parked in the driveway, I was now filled with fear and panic. I walked quietly past the car, hoping the man who was leaning against the driver's-side door and smoking a cigarette would not see me. It was Lenny, my mother's boyfriend.

I stopped in my tracks as I opened the door and went inside. Mrs. Giaimo was arguing in the living room. Then I heard her voice.

Amy was arguing with Mrs. Giaimo. "SHE'S MY DAUGHTER AND I'M TAKING HER OUT OF HERE NOW."

"You can't just come in my house and take Sandy out of here!" yelled Mrs. Giaimo.

The room became silent, but only for a moment, when each noticed me standing in the room. "Sandy, get your things. You're getting out of here now!" Amy demanded.

I looked to Mrs. Giaimo. I saw the pain and anger in her face. I wanted to tell her at that moment how much she meant to me, how much I loved her. But my mother was here. I dared not speak.

The ringing telephone sent Mrs. Giaimo moving to answer it.

"Yes, I heard you," and then she hung up the telephone.

Ms. Foyer had called to confirm that I was to go with Amy.

I turned toward the bedroom, knowing that the look on Catherine's face meant only one thing—I was leaving. My clothes were gathered and placed in paper bags. Amy grabbed what she could carry to the door, and yelled for Lenny to come put my things in the car. Lenny put his foot in the door.

"I won't have that strange man in my house. You take the things outside to him," spoke Mrs. Giaimo.

I followed Amy out the door. Fighting back the tears, I glanced back. Catherine was livid as she cried out, "You'd better take care of Sandy."

The Giaimo family will always be remembered with my deepest appreciation for all the love and care they showed me. I can't thank them enough for giving me the opportunity to see what a loving family was all about.

[handwritten margin note: mum picks up Sandy to take her home]

Chapter Five—Despair

HOLDING MY BREATH, I climbed past Amy to get in the car. She and the car reeked of alcohol and cigarette smoke. Sitting quietly in the back seat, I tried not to feel and pushed any thoughts of the past or future from my mind. I could only faintly hear Amy's voice coming from the front of the car as we drove away. Not wanting to think that I might never see the Giaimo family again, I split off and blocked everything out.

Amy worked nights as a barmaid—sleeping the booze off during the day. She reminded me every chance she got of how much trouble she had gone through to get us kids back—five years later. In her drunken state of mind, she would tell us about how lucky we were to have her for a mother, "after all I've done for you kids."

I didn't know how to make her stop drinking, or how to make her happy. I flipped in and out of wanting to help her, and wishing she were dead. Why did it take her five years to get us back? We were less than ten miles away. Why didn't she come to visit more often?

The car pulled up in front of a small apartment complex on the east side of Cleveland. It was quite a difference from the neighborhood and house I had just left. Amy's voice interrupted my thoughts. "Well, this is it. Get your stuff and come on. I haven't got all day. I was supposed to be at work an hour ago."

Amy remained in the car with Lenny. She leaned forward and held the front seat back so I could get out of the car. While I struggled with the bags of clothes, Lenny spoke only to say, "See you later kiddo." I despised him. What gave him the right to call me "kiddo?"

Without looking at either of them, I got out of the car and walked toward the apartment door Mother had pointed out. I pushed the apartment door open cautiously and stood in the living room. I didn't know what to expect once inside. But this was certainly not it. It was a small, three-room apartment. A double bed filled the only bedroom. Albert, Mario, and Sam shared the bed. The sofa in the living room opened out into a bed, which I was to share with Amy.

Just as I was beginning to wonder where the boys were, I could hear the voices and laughter of the boys coming in behind me. I hated myself for not being more cheerful. The boys had long ago named me "Queenie." They made fun of the frilly dresses and ribbons they saw me in on visiting days at the foster home. I tried to shrug off my disgust at the appearance of the apartment and tried to be happy, at least for being with the boys again.

Mario tackled me, pushing me to the floor, and laughed. "Hey Sis."

Albert and Sam didn't seem to care or give much notice to my being there and went to the refrigerator, looking for something to eat. Amy was still out in front and yelled from the car, "Now, I want you kids to behave and stay put. Don't leave this apartment!"

She drove away and did not return until early morning.

The boys went wild. "Yea! She's gone," Albert responded as he reached into his worn out jacket pocket and pulled out a package of Pall Mall cigarettes. He started passing them around. "Sandy, you want one?" he asked, holding the pack out to me.

"No, I don't! And I'm going to tell on you."

They just laughed at me and lit the cigarettes anyway. "All right—party time!" one of them yelled out.

Amy had picked the boys up from Parmadale a few days earlier, so they had a few days to see what life was going to be like. I sat down, not knowing whether to laugh or cry. Everything was moving so fast.

The reality of Angelo being sent to prison while we were in Parmadale wasn't fully understood, but I did understand he had stopped visiting us. Angelo always referred to this time as "being away at college." Later, we were given several different versions of the events that led up to his arrest.

Amy's version of the story was: "I was at home, sleeping alone one night when your father came in drunk and poured liquid acid over my body, aiming mostly between my legs."

Angelo had his own version: "I came home one night after working all day and found your mother in bed with her boyfriend, Lenny." And this was said in such a matter-of-fact, justified manner that we dared not question him on his actions.

Amy was hospitalized for several months. The acid had burned her body, exposing the bone in some areas. Parts of her hands were burned as she reached down in agony to the burning in her inner thighs. Amy endured many skin-graft operations and the doctors were not sure if she would ever walk again. The surgeries were successful. She has never recovered emotionally however. And as soon as she was able to walk, her drinking accelerated. Leaving the hospital without medical consent, Amy proceeded to take a cab to the nearest bar where she drank and told anyone who would listen, "Look what he did to me."

As the years passed, I heard countless times when she was in her really pitiful and incomprehensible moods, "Look what your father did to me!"

I was sickened and felt sorry for her public—as well as private—displays in which she would go through the ritual of pulling her pants down and repeating the same story. "Now, you want to know why I drink? Wouldn't you drink if you looked like me?"

Angelo blamed Mother. Amy blamed Father.

Lenny was a regular at the bar where Amy was working and each night, while she worked, he sat drinking and watched over her. They had been dating for the last couple of years. It was Lenny who convinced Amy to get her children out of Parmadale and the foster homes.

We stayed only a short while in the apartment until Lenny had persuaded Amy that the three-room apartment was no place to raise four children. He bought a two-story house with a large backyard and moved us all in with him. Hillbilly music played on the record player.

One of their favorite songs was "Dang-em, Oughta Take a Rope and Hang-em."

Their relationship, like all of my mother's relationships, didn't last. Lenny tried his best to endure the rocky relationship, often telling us he loved us kids but didn't know how long he could put up with "your mother."

Lenny certainly thought more of us than our own father. But he tired of Amy's drinking and all the fighting between them. Even though he stopped seeing Amy after we had all moved out of his house, the boys and I continued to visit him when we were in the neighborhood. Lenny's mother was also very kind to us, feeding us whenever we stopped in to see her. Lenny and his mother always asked about Amy.

We moved from place to place, not staying in one apartment for more than a few months. Amy was not responsible enough to pay the bills, and we were evicted often. Drinking always came first. After living in foster homes and seeing how other people lived, I felt so ashamed of our apartment and living conditions.

We never saw much of Mother. When we did, we learned to tolerate her demented behavior, knowing she would either leave the house or pass out soon.

Amy was not approachable. The only time I had any physical contact from her was after she had passed out on the couch and I curled up next to her. At these moments, shutting the world out, I pretended all was well. But the image was shattered by the voices of the adults in my life. I often heard relatives say things like, "Isn't it a shame? Amy is such an attractive-looking woman, but . . . "

Amy was drunk most of the time. I despised her. I hated her for what she was doing to herself, the boys, and to me. I didn't want to look like her, or be like her. Embarrassed that she was a barmaid, that she got drunk, and that she was bringing strange men home with her, I kept to myself at school, embarrassed to make friends or bring anyone home.

Amy's behavior with the men she brought home was relentless. "Sandy, come over here and give Uncle . . . a kiss." How could she humiliate me this way or even consider such a thing? I knew these guys were not my uncles. And even if they were, why would I kiss them—why would she?

I refused to degrade myself, but I also feared her getting angry at me. Amy was quick, harsh, and loud in her manner of speaking, "Because I said so!" Not wanting to argue with her, I simply left the room.

One night one of these men whom she brought home was lying on the couch. As I tried to pass him heading into the kitchen, he jumped up and made a game out of grabbing hold of me. I was furious and pulled my face away as he tried to slobber kisses on my face. He mumbled in his whiskey breath and told me how beautiful I was going to be, that I looked just like my mother. Amy spoke up jokingly: "Oh, you better leave her alone. She thinks she's better than everyone else."

The boys ran the streets until all hours of the night. I dreaded staying home alone. They allowed me to tag along after much begging to let me go with them. After the usual "No, you're a girl!" I would eventually be allowed to follow them.

The neighbors and local business owners did not appreciate our outings. We stole candy and cigarettes from the various corner markets. We sanded pennies down on the concrete and put them in the pinball machines as dimes. We stole eggs, only to throw them at passing cars from the bridge. We knocked on doors, and when the door was opened we threw the eggs inside and ran.

The whole point of the game was to anger someone enough that they would chase us. We were the brats that belonged to "that woman who's never home to look after those kids."

We were evicted, once again, and forced to move. This time it was winter, and we moved into a duplex. The apartment was extremely run down and we were the only tenants living in it. It was so cold at night, and Amy did not have money for coal to fuel the furnace. So while she was out, my brothers and I did whatever we could to stay warm. This meant gathering up wood—anything made of wood. We proceeded to burn doors that divided other apartments from ours, wooden kitchen chairs, and an old television cabinet. Somehow these items were never missed. When all else failed we left the oven on and the door open—the four gas burners going at night, trying to heat the place. It never occurred to us that we might have set the place on fire.

For food, Mario and I went into the local market. While I stood chatting to the store owner, Mario gathered up and hid whatever food items he could steal under his coat. Then, picking up a single loaf of bread, he carried it over to the counter and asked the store owner to put it on our credit account while he asked me if "mom" wanted us to get anything else.

"No, Mario," I replied. Then we ran home, laughing together.

I never could understand how Albert and Mario seemed to always have money. Then one night I awoke and heard them quarreling in the kitchen. Moving closer to the door so I could listen, I quietly looked around the door. The boys sat on the floor next to a wallet, dividing up the money. "Where did you get that money?" I demanded as I entered the room.

"Be quiet! Do you want to wake them up?" Albert asked.

"What are you two doing?"

"If you promise not to tell, we'll cut you in."

"What are you talking about?" I asked again.

"Well, you see . . . " Mario paused. "You know the guys that mom brings home with her? After they pass out, we collect a little money for ourselves."

My brothers were always up to something. Whenever I needed money all I had to do was keep an eye on them. Sooner or later, I would catch them doing something and they would pay me off to keep quiet about it.

Survival came first. I learned to steal food and clothes. We didn't attend school on a regular basis. I had the feeling that everyone was talking about me or my family. I became more and more anxious and irritated. I tried to keep our apartment as orderly as possible, considering I had three brothers who couldn't seem to care less about anything.

The boys had frequent parties while Mother was out. The place would fill with kids from the neighborhood—ranging from age thirteen through sixteen—knowing there would be no supervision at the Cicero house. When stealing booze was a problem, they resorted to sniffing airplane glue from a paper bag. I pretended to be sniffing glue right along with them, just so I could fit in—and to keep them from calling me names or making fun of me. Eventually, I would become tired of the party and my brothers' friends, and go upstairs to bed. Not owning any pajamas, I always crawled into bed, still dressed, and rocked myself to sleep.

One particular night around ten o'clock, I awoke in a sudden panic as my wrist was being pulled down on top of clammy, wrinkled flesh. I tried to scream for help. Nothing came out. I began twisting my body, trying to free myself from his grip. He pulled me closer, wrapping his legs around mine. One hand rubbed my not-yet-developed chest while the other hand moved roughly toward my thighs and pulled at my pants, trying to remove them. As I desperately tried to free myself from him, he mumbled in my ear: "Come on, honey. Don't you want to feel good? Take off your pants."

The man again forced my hand to touch his soft penis. Pushing him away with every ounce of strength in my eleven-year-old frame, I failed again in my attempt to call for help—only a gasp would come out. Struggling to get free, I twisted and turned away from him, pushing with both feet—hands against the wall.

I managed to push the twin bed far enough away from the wall to create a space for me as he let go of his hold on me while reaching to remove his own pants. I quickly dropped to the floor and crawled under the bed, and then hurried out of the room and darted into the bathroom across the hall for safety. Racing to shut and lock the door, I turned, leaning with my back pressed against the door. I couldn't quiet my pounding heart. It was beating so fast now I was afraid he would hear me. Pressing my ear to the door, I tried listening for the sound of the man in the hall. His voice broke through me like a knife. Trembling, and holding my breath, I listened as the man outside the door pleaded with me to open it.

I did not respond.

He begged me to let him in because he needed to go to the bathroom!

After I heard his voice, I realized who the stranger was. I had seen him several times with my mother. I continued to keep silent and waited for Edward to go away.

Still too frightened to move, I stayed pressed against the door. In frozen terror, my mind kept playing tricks on me. I had to keep my wits about me. The mere sound of my own breathing terrified me. Fighting to stay alert, I kept slipping in and out of reality—splitting off and having my mind go blank from fear. I knew I must somehow get out of the bathroom and go for help. With each movement, the fear shot through me and I wondered if he heard me. I slowly and carefully unlocked the door. I stopped to listen again—nothing. Turning the handle and releasing the catch, I stopped to listen—nothing. Careful as I began to pull the door open and guarding myself behind it, I tried to focus in the darkness as I looked up and down the hall— no sight of anyone.

I moved quickly into the boys' bedroom and shook Mario, in a low whisper. "Mario, get up. I need your help."

No response. Again, I shook him.

Grumbling he commanded, "Get out of here."

"Mario, you have to help me," I pleaded.

"Go away," he mumbled.

I gave up, not wanting him to make any noise. Once downstairs, I hurried to the telephone. It was dark in the room and I had trouble dialing the number. I tried to reach Mother by telephoning the bar. "Amy, please hurry!" I demanded abruptly.

The voice on the other end of the receiver did not care for the interruption or the tone of my voice. He snapped back at me, "Amy no longer works here." And he proceeded to hang up before I could speak again.

I hung up the phone and sat down on the couch. It was almost 2 a.m.

Sometime later, I heard Amy coming up the sidewalk to the apartment. Startled by the sound of a man's voice with her, I panicked and jumped to hide behind the overstuffed chair in the living room.

They came through the kitchen and entered the living room. Every sound seemed amplified. Amy opened the sofa sleeper and both bodies fell down onto the bed. I peeked around the chair to see what was going on, only to see them tearing at each other to remove their clothing. Quickly moving back out of sight, I tried not to breathe and covered my ears, hoping to block out the noises they made. I could still hear springs squeaking as they bounced up and down. The grunts and groans and the sound of flesh rubbing flesh sickened me. Tears ran down my face with the fear of being caught. I didn't move.

Splitting off from them, I focused on how I was going to get out of the room without being seen or heard.

The room got quiet. I waited to see if they had gone to sleep—no such luck. Just as I was about to move, I heard the person she was with saying he had to get going. Within minutes, Amy got up to walk him to the kitchen door. Seizing the opportunity, I hurried out from behind the chair. There was no way I could get past her and up the stairs without being seen.

My legs were shaky and I sat down on the edge of the bed. Closing the door, Mother turned around and saw me. "What the hell are you doing? And why aren't you in bed?" she scolded.

Choked up, with tears streaming down my face, I cried out softly, "Edward tried to rape me!"

I didn't really understand fully what I had said. I had heard my brothers making fun of Mother and the guys she brought home. I had been cautioned once or twice by neighbors to be careful. "With all those boys in your house that your brothers bring home, you could end up getting yourself raped." Through the sobs, I tried to explain to her what took place—only to have her cut me off and order me to "Stop your crying. I'll take care of him."

Amy picked up the telephone and tried calling his apartment. No answer. Again I tried to speak. And again she told me, "Quit your crying and go to bed."

"Well, he's not home," she announced. "But I'll take care of this tomorrow when I see him. Didn't I tell you to get to bed?"

Shaking my head, "But, I can't!" I cried out.

"Why not?" she demanded.

"Because he's upstairs, passed out in my bed."

I had seen his body lying on my bed when I crept past the door on my way downstairs.

Amy sprang out of the chair and headed up the stairs, still naked as she entered my room. "Honey, Edward." She nudged gently at his bare shoulder while she sat on the edge of my bed. He rolled over and reached up for her. His hand began roaming over her naked breast while she explained, "You know anytime you want anything, all you have to do is ask."

I was shocked and furious. How could my mother speak to him in such a soft, gentle voice? Why wasn't my mother trying to comfort me? Why was she speaking so nicely to this guy who tried to rape her daughter? Amy was not aware that I had followed her up the stairs. Now standing in the hallway, in front of the door, I shook my head in disbelief, screaming out, "You bitch!"—but only in my head. Frustrated and livid, I kept silent. Her voice in my head kept repeating the same words each time I wanted to speak out. "If you brats want to— you can just go back to Parmadale." I turned and ran down the stairs as fast as my legs could carry me. Once outside, I continued to run— running until, one more time, I realized I had nowhere to go.

Tony was home on leave from the army. He was a stranger to me. Even though we had the same father, he had only lived with Angelo, Amy, the boys and me until I was about four. We had not lived under the same roof since. Tony was seven years older than I was. His cocky, arrogant ways left me feeling awkward and uncomfortable around him. Yet, as always, I was the one confused and questioning my own feelings. I hated being so afraid. Why couldn't I be more like everyone else in the family? Mother certainly showed no fear of anyone. My brothers, with the exception of Sam, all fought back on occasion—only to be slapped down by Mother. Tony was a mystery to me, and yet I looked up to him.

Tony's sudden appearance on the scene came as a surprise. He paced around in the kitchen and ordered me, "Get yourself cleaned up and put on something decent to wear. I have someone coming over to the house that I want you to meet."

I was hurt by his comments and couldn't understand why he was suddenly so interested in me. Instincts told me I wasn't to trust him. Wondering to myself as I walked up the stairs, I did as I was told. But I also grumbled to myself, "What gives him the right to walk in here after all these years and start telling me what to do?"

What he didn't tell me was that while visiting the bar where Amy worked, he overheard the story of the incident involving Edward. Only he heard the version being told from a drunk sitting at the bar: "Hey! Did you hear about the barmaid's daughter being raped?" He was outraged and—whether to defend me, or looking for a fight which was his m.o.—he succeeded only in stirring up trouble for me.

Weeks had now passed, possibly a month. I had pushed the whole occurrence out of my mind.

When I came down the stairs, I heard Tony talking to a couple of men. Stopping at the bottom of the steps, I now saw that he was talking with two cops in the kitchen. Tony looked at me and instructed me, "Sandy, go ahead and tell the police what happened to you!"

I stood there, wide-eyed and stunned. "What are you talking about?" I questioned.

"Cut the crap, Sandy. Tell them what Edward did to you!"

Who had told him? Why was he doing this to me? I was outraged. I stood motionless. Before anyone had a chance to question me further, Amy walked into the kitchen. Slamming the kitchen door behind her, she glared at Tony and asked, "What the hell is going on here? And who the hell called you?" as she looked to the cops.

"Calm down, Amy," one of them answered.

I was watching the police as they spoke to Mother—irked that they didn't even need to ask her name. Working at the bars in Cleveland and giving booze away freely after hours, everyone seemed to know Amy on a first-name basis, and knew tips were a must.

"We have a complaint filed by your son, concerning your daughter."

Amy walked over to one of the cops. "Come with me."

They walked into the living room. Amy now stood only inches from him and whispered in his ear. They laughed. She patted his ass and they came back to the kitchen. "Let's go," he said to his partner. And they left.

Amy looked at Tony. "Get out! I don't need any more trouble around here."

Tony's face turned bright red and his veins were popping out of the side of his neck. "You can go to hell, slut!"

He raced out of the kitchen, slamming the door behind him. Amy turned without even looking my way and said, "I have to get back to work."

And with that she walked out. They were all gone now, leaving me alone in the kitchen. It was a few months before the incident was to be mentioned again.

Tony was furious, and he decided to go after Edward himself. He had heard that Edward was still hanging around Amy at the bar where she now worked. Tony walked into the bar and started asking questions of the other patrons. "Hey, do you know a guy named Edward?"

"Yeah, that's him at the end of the bar next to Amy."

Tony looked over and in an instant moved across the room toward Edward. Amy moved back as Tony slammed the barstool across Edward's back, splitting his forehead open when his head hit the counter in front of him. Edward was taken to the hospital for stitches, and Tony went back to the army.

But before he left he went to visit Angelo in prison. He told Angelo about the boyfriend of Amy's who had raped me. Tony, like everyone else, had not believed me—or did not want to believe me—when I told him nothing happened, that I managed to get away from Edward.

Tony returned to duty, and it was two years before I was to see him again. Meanwhile, life for me remained the same.

Jeri Bain became my only friend in school—well, at least when we were in school. We began ditching classes and hanging out in the alley across the street from the school with other kids who were doing the same. We just hung out, smoking and playing big shots. Sometimes, one of the older boys would steal a car and we'd all pile in and go joy-riding for the day.

Jeri was worried about going home one day after learning the truant officers had called Mrs. Bain and reported that she had not been attending school. She told me she just couldn't go home and face her mother, and asked me to run away with her.

Claiming she had an aunt in West Virginia, she said that we could go and stay with her. And with little thought of any more details, we were off together—following the railroad tracks out of town. We walked until dusk. Our legs and feet grew tired. And we were both hungry. Jeri suggested we get over to the main highway and hitchhike the rest of the way.

The first couple of rides went okay. The next ride, however, was with a guy who traveled the way Mother did. He stopped often. "I'll be right back—just going to run in here for one drink."

Jeri was not accustomed to waiting in cars. I assured her it would be all right. "My mother does this all the time." And we waited for him to return.

Jeri and I had made a pact with each other that we would take turns in the front seat on each ride. It was now my turn for the front seat. When he finally returned from the bar, he got in the car and moved over toward me. Grabbing hold of my shoulder and pulling me to him, he pressed his lips to mine. I tried to push him away. He just laughed at me as he moved back to the driver's side. "Oh, you want to play hard-to-get? Okay! I'll wait until we get to the hotel, girls."

Once on the road, I looked back at Jeri and nodded toward the door. As soon as the car came to a stop for a red light, I threw open my car door and yelled for Jeri to get out. We kept on running until we couldn't run any more.

Hungry and tired, Jeri walked with me around the small town of Canton, Ohio. We had been on the run since early morning and here we were, ten hours later, only about forty miles outside of Cleveland. . We entered the local market without money. We thought we were careful in the store, hiding the food we wanted under our coats. But once outside the door we found out differently.

The "black and white" rolled to a stop in front of us. The officers stepped out of the police car and held the back door open as one told us both to get in the car. Jeri and I refused to give them our real names—this was part of our original plan.

Parmadale had prepared me for the kind of treatment we received. The policewoman stood in the showers with a hose, spraying us with some sort of disinfectant. This was no big deal to me, I pretended. Jeri cried from the humiliation and fear. We were put in separate rooms. I was put in with three other girls who tried to scare me with horror stories of how I could forget about ever getting out of this place. I didn't care and went to sleep.

It was three o'clock in the morning when the door opened. A policewoman stood in the doorway and told me to follow her. I dressed while she stood watching. Then she led me to the lobby area.

When I entered the room, Amy glanced in my direction briefly as she continued signing papers for my release. She was such an embarrassment to me—black stretch pants, light sweater, gold slippers, and red lipstick and nail polish. Her hair was dyed jet-black, teased and piled high on her head. It was obvious she had been drinking.

"Well, Mrs. Cicero. Here she is," the guard announced. "We are not sure why she ran away from home. That girl has not spoken a word since we brought her in last night."

I broke my silence, responding boldly. "You've met my mother and you still want to know why I ran away?" With that remark, Amy whipped around and slapped me across the face.

I understood by now that I would be slapped whether or not I spoke and began mouthing off whenever the opportunity presented itself. Her favorite technique seemed to be to walk up to me and slap me across the face, at the same time snapping, "Get that look off your face! You look just like your father."

Life continued, with Amy keeping late hours or not returning at all. We had been living with her for almost a year now.

One morning, as I passed the hallway window, I noticed a car pulling in the driveway and stopping next to the duplex in front of ours. It was a yellow cab. I watched in wonder as the cab door opened. We didn't know anyone who could afford to take a cab.

Angelo stepped out. The whiteness of the snow on the ground made his shiny black shoes stand out. I watched Angelo for a moment as he knocked on the neighbor's door. Turning from the window, I ran to warn the boys, "Get up you guys. Dad's here." Amy had divorced Angelo in 1963 while he was serving his sentence in the State Correctional Institution—charged with malicious assault.

I was coming down the stairs to the kitchen as he walked in.

Without even greeting us, Angelo went over to the stove and mumbled to himself, "How stupid can anyone be?" as he turned the burners on the stove off.

I stopped on the bottom step and waited to see what he was doing. He turned and said to me, "What the hell are you damned kids doing in here with the gas burners on and the oven door open?"

Without answering, I looked down toward the floor. Hurt that he didn't seem happy to see me, I answered in a low voice, "It gets so cold in here at night. We're just trying to get some heat in here."

Mario started down the stairs behind me, but stopped when he heard what was going on. Angelo yelled up the stairs, "Mario, get down here. And tell your brothers to get their asses down here too!"

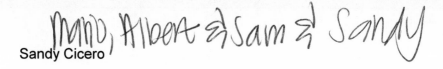
Albert and Sam came out of the bedroom, still half-asleep and wondering what was going on. We had not seen Angelo all these years, and we had not bothered to write him since we had gotten out of Parmadale.

He wasted no time in dictating orders. Angelo had been paroled into the custody of his mother. Now, he stood there, telling us "Your mother is no damn good. Get whatever you want and let's get out of this dump. And hurry up; I have a cab waiting outside."

Within weeks of his release from prison, Angelo took Amy to court to gain custody of us—charging her with child neglect, and pointing out that one of her boyfriends had raped me. Believing him, the court agreed to give a newly paroled man custody of four young children.

Once again, Angelo got to anger Amy by taking us away—this time for good. We saw nor heard little of her from that day on. While in the orphanage or foster homes, a social worker came by to check in on us monthly. But once we were returned to our parents, the case was closed. No Ms. Foyer, or any other social worker, came to the house again to check on us—to see how we were doing.

Chapter Six—The Con Man

AFTER GRANDPA DIED, the family insisted that Grandma Cicero should not live alone. One of the daughters and her husband moved in soon afterward.

Uncle Ozzie and Aunt Laura were shocked when they heard the news—not only was Angelo moving in, but he had persuaded Grandma that the house was big enough for his four kids.

Ozzie was a grandiose man. He walked swiftly, as though going to some place of importance—even if that meant to the kitchen. When they first were married, they lived and owned a neighborhood tavern in New York. Ozzie's drinking caused them to lose the bar and shortly afterward they moved to Cleveland. Ozzie now worked sixteen hours a day as a security guard for two different companies.

It seemed that Laura's life was just something to be endured. They never had children of their own, suffering a great deal after losing several babies through miscarriages. At the time when Angelo was giving out his children, they had taken Tony in and raised him until he went into the army. Laura worked five or six days a week for over twenty years as a seamstress.

The boys shared the upstairs attic area, which had been converted into an extra large bedroom. I shared a small downstairs bedroom with Grandma Rosa, and we slept together in a double bed. The only other item that fit into the narrow room was a small dresser. I didn't

[handwritten margin notes: "aunt & uncle", "more ie with dad, Grandma, brothers", "Grandpa dies →"]

mind sharing a room with Rosa. In fact, I enjoyed sleeping next to her. She smelled good, and it was very comforting to be near her.

The summer nights in Cleveland left everyone edgy and miserable from the heat and humidity. Tossing and turning one evening, I asked permission from Grandma to make a tent out of a sheet and set it up in the backyard, smiling as she agreed to locate an older, worn sheet and let me have it. The clothesline served to hold up the sheet.

I was so proud and excited to have built a tent all by myself! I would have to wait till morning to show it off to the boys. They were sound asleep upstairs.

Not long after climbing under the sheet and inside the tent, Angelo pushed back the opening. He wanted to see how I was doing.

"Sandy?" he spoke mushily. "Sure is cooler out here. Would you mind if I joined you?" he asked.

I was so proud of my tent and pleased to show it off. I also liked the idea of having my dad around after all the years of separation. I enjoyed the attention and was pleased to have him back in my life.

He told me how much he missed me, and how he was going to make it up to me. I tried to convince him that it didn't matter, that I was just glad he was home now. He took hold of my hand, telling me how sorry he was for not being there for us; and how much he missed me; and that things were going to be different from now on. He told me I was "daddy's little girl" and that I didn't have to worry any more—he would take care of me from now on.

Angelo lit a cigarette and lay back, putting his free arm around me. He lay close to me as he finished the cigarette. I was about to drift into sleep when Angelo started asking me questions about Amy—questioning me about the guy who took advantage of me and wanting to know the details of what had happened.

I began to panic and held my breath—once again trying to push all thoughts from my memory. Why do I have to go over this again? How had he heard about it anyway?

"Sandy, don't be afraid. I want to know what happened," he persisted.

I hoped that if I lay there without moving he would think I was asleep and leave me alone. I was wrong. "Well, Sandy, talk to me. I am your father. And, as your father, it is my duty to check you to make sure you are okay!"

What was he talking about—check me—my mind wondered, trying to come up with some kind of answer.

"Nothing happened," I whimpered.

"Now, don't lie to me, Sandy. I want you to turn over on your back," he ordered as he gently but firmly tried to pull me over. My body tensed in an attempt to resist, but he pulled firmer and succeeded in getting me on my back. I was too afraid to cry. I fought back the tears. "Nothing happened. I got away from him. Why won't anyone believe me?" I pleaded.

"Well then, if nothing happened you won't mind me checking you."

I was twelve years old. I had no idea what he meant by "checking me." Frightened and confused, somehow I managed to shut down and split off all emotions and lay frozen while he forced himself slowly inside of me. I listened to the crickets in the distance and his whispers telling me it was because he loved me, and he didn't want anyone to hurt me—that it was his duty as my father to check me.

I do not know how long it was before Angelo got up and left the tent. Without looking back or commenting, he returned to the house. I rocked silently, feeling the stickiness between my legs—fearing morning and life in a whole new way.

A forty-year-old man was imprisoned for brutally attacking his wife and upon release from serving a prison sentence, he gains custody of four children. He was known for his alcohol and drug abuse and had been hospitalized for mental illness. Yet, because he had served his time sitting in a cell, he was now considered "reformed" and able to be trusted with the care of children.

Within weeks of being allowed to "take care" of us, he was not only drinking daily, but verbally and physically abusing his sons while sexually molesting his daughter.

Among Angelo's many personalities was a hypochondriac. He managed to convince several doctors to prescribe a variety of medications. He even went as far as to obtain a copy of the Physicians Desk Reference guide and studied it for symptoms to relate to the doctor to get the pill he wanted.

had marked here! ?

I fell for another one of his acts for attention. We had not been living with him for more than a month or so. One day I found him lying in bed with the blanket tucked up under his chin. I thought he was sleeping. I went to close the bedroom door.

He groaned.

"Are you okay?" I responded.

"Sandy. Is that my Sandy?" he said in a barely audible sound.

"Yes."

"Come here. Come closer," he moaned again.

My heart went out to him. He was obviously in a lot of pain. He took hold of my hand after I sat down on the bed next to him. He began again, speaking slowly and dropping off into a trance-like state, pleading with me not to leave him alone. He said he didn't want to die alone.

I wanted to run for help. Everyone else in the household was outside enjoying the Labor Day weekend. He tightened his grip on my hand. "Don't go."

The telephone began ringing in the outer room. Uncle Ozzie yelled in through the kitchen window, "Hey, you guys. Isn't anybody going to answer that phone?"

Father let go of my hand, nodding to me to go ahead and get the phone. I raced to the ringing phone and tried to explain that Father was too sick to come to the phone.

Just as I continued to explain further, Angelo grabbed the receiver from me. He spoke in a strong voice and agreed to the caller that, yes, he would have the children at the school on Monday morning. The school called about transferring the boys and me into the new school district. I was shocked and angry!

Crying out, I said "How could you do this to me? How could you let me think you were dying?"

No response. And then he grinned at me. "I was just kidding around. Can't your own father kid around with you without you taking everything so serious?"

Uncle Ozzie was either working or sleeping, so we did not see much of each other. Aunt Laura was not so lucky. After working eight hours a day, she returned home each night on the bus to find Angelo drinking and his children running wild in and out of the house. She usually ended up arguing with Angelo before Rosa stepped in to break it up.

Laura could not tolerate the living arrangements any longer, and convinced her husband and Rosa that they should move out. Moving out meant moving just down the block into a two-bedroom duplex apartment. Grandma went with them, leaving the house to Angelo. The summer heat in the attic was unbearable, and the boys were happy to have a bedroom downstairs. I kept Grandma's room.

Angelo was drinking daily. While the relatives still lived in the house, he tried to hide his drinking by doing it in the basement or out in the backyard. Now, with the house to himself, he could drink anywhere he pleased.

The only one he hid his drinking from was the parole officer. Drinking was considered a violation of his parole and he would have been sent back to prison if caught. If only I had realized the possibilities then. I guess the fear of the unknown was greater than the fear of living with my father. Each move in my life, so far, had certainly not felt like an improvement. I knew Angelo was right on one thing. If I did blow the whistle on him, the boys and I would be separated and sent away again to some sort of institution.

Angelo hid in the basement whenever a car pulled in the driveway. He used me to open the door to any visitors. My job was to signal when the caller was gone by stomping my foot on the floor.

It was no use trying to question or confront him. Angelo had an answer, a look, and would scream with the veins popping out in his neck, "When you're in my house, you'll do as I say!"

Mario and I walked slowly down the street toward Ozzie and Laura's. We hated going, but knew we must do as we were told. We sat sulking in their kitchen, waiting for them to fill the paper bags. I did not understand, and criticized Laura and Ozzie harshly. I was twelve years old and only saw them when sent on a mission for food or money because dad was too drunk to work and support us. If they had a problem with giving, why didn't they tell Angelo about it or stop doing it? Why did they grudgingly pack up a paper bag of bread and lunch meat, while spouting off to me and Mario about "what a no-good bum your father is"?

I really was getting tired of hearing "you kids," "your mother," "your father."

One of Angelo's sisters came to the house occasionally to bring not only hand-me-down clothes from her children, but also a friendly face. She never looked down on us children. Then one day she stopped coming. She was killed in a car accident—hit by a drunk driver on her way to church.

Angelo convinced me that it was because I was so special that he taught me to drive. Now, I knew that he did this, not because he wanted to be "Father of the Year," but because he was too drunk to get himself home. He also loved pressing the rules in life. I learned to drive at the age of thirteen, so I could drop him off or pick him up at the local bars. I did enjoy driving. It made me feel grown up. This was one thing I could do that my brothers couldn't. They could go out to the playground, but I could drive the car sometimes.

Once, while I was driving him home from the bar, we approached a stop sign and the brakes failed. Angelo was passed out on the front seat.

"Damn."

I tried pumping the brakes several times. When I realized it was no use, I held my breath, closed my eyes, and drove into the car in front of us. Angelo sat up and looked around to see what the bang was. Slurring his words, he ordered me to "Get out of the car!"

We were standing on the sidewalk when the police arrived. Angelo was taken to jail for drunk driving. No one bothered to check if he had an arrest record, and they released him the next day after he sobered up. I was let go, after lying that I could walk home from there and my mother would be waiting.

Another experience involved me driving up in front of the neighborhood teenagers who were hanging out at a corner deli. One of the boys started to approach the car when he saw what he thought was a young, attractive girl at the steering wheel. I threw up my arms, waving and trying to signal him to stay away from the car. But he continued. Leaning in on the passenger side, I saw the grin on the boy's face vanish. Angelo was not passed out. The gun barrel was now pressed into his face and he barked, "What the hell do you want?"

Angelo carried his sawed-off shotgun with him under the seat of the car. I had not seen him reach for it. I did a lot of nervous begging in those days. "Dear God, if you're there, please don't let him shoot this guy."

The police came to our door on many occasions; if not for the boys, then looking for Angelo. I answered the door one day and told them he wasn't home. The police said they wanted to question him about his whereabouts that afternoon. He had been reported for entering a bar with a gun.

Angelo had gone into a bar in a part of town known as the Polish Village, where they didn't like or want people who were not of the same ethnic background. Angelo walked in anyway when he wanted a drink. He was not a big man. His medium-sized build was not threatening, and he moved slowly. Inside the bar, he stood and ordered a drink. Suddenly, there was an outburst in the room. A voice cried out, "We don't serve Wops!"

Without saying a word, Angelo turned and walked out of the bar. The noise and laughter drummed in his ears. He returned within minutes, firing a shot into the air. He got their attention. "On the floor, all you damn Polacks! Oh yeah, by the way, you can also buy me a few drinks."

He made them kneel while he sat drinking. Angelo finished his drinks and thanked them for their hospitality. Leaving them on the floor, he walked out.

I neither liked nor disliked dogs, and I didn't pay much attention to the new boxer puppy that Tony gave us after he discovered he was not allowed to keep the dog in his apartment. The boys, however, named the dog Sam and enjoyed playing and wrestling on the floor with it.

We were responsible for feeding and cleaning up after the dog if we wanted to keep him. Also, we put the dog in the basement before we left the house. Upon returning home one day, we discovered that the puppy had somehow freed himself from the basement or was left upstairs when we left. No one would have ever admitted to such an error to Angelo. The puppy had knocked over the kitchen trash can, scattering its contents around the room. Now, he was chewing on the wooden leg of a living room chair.

Angelo's mood swings and temper were becoming increasingly unbearable. He went into a rage when he saw what the puppy was doing. Angelo grabbed him by his collar. The poor thing let out a yelp. Picking him up off the floor and dangling him in the air, he carried it into the kitchen. The boys and I watched in horror as he pulled a knife from the drawer. I screamed for Angelo to stop, but it was too late. He proceeded to stab the dog in the chest. We were too terrified to move. He dropped the dog to the floor, kicking him under the table. After Angelo walked out of the kitchen and sat down in his chair, we moved quickly to reach for the dog. He lay on his side as the blood poured out of the open wound. Mario reached to pick up the dog, but Angelo yelled, "Put that damn dog down or the same thing will happen to you!"

We knew he meant what he said. We knew what he had done to Amy and we watched him kill two other dogs—one he left in the basement to starve to death; the other died from severe blows to the head.

All the neighbors ever saw was a single, handsome, and well-groomed man struggling along to provide for his children. They greeted him warmly, always with a smile.

But as Angelo's children we lived in constant fear of him.

I had no privacy. Angelo marched into whatever room I was in, whenever he was moved to do so. We were not permitted to lock doors. He made regular visits to the bathroom to check in on me while I was taking a bath, or to wash my back—letting his hands roam to other parts. And I was supposed to find this amusing, as though it was a slip on his part. I knew how brutal and capable of killing he was. Fear kept me silent.

But the loathing continued to grow inside of me. First the nuns, and now my father thinks I can't take a bath without supervision. I felt as if I was losing my mind. Fighting hopelessness and rage, I took the alcohol Angelo offered to me with little hesitation. He explained to me that he only wanted me "to learn how to drink like a lady, so you won't turn out like your mother."

Each night, he sat me down at the kitchen table—sometimes before the boys returned from the playground, but mostly after they were sent to bed. He poured whiskey into a small glass for me.

I had collected the glasses from jelly jars. I remember staring at the colorful cartoon characters on the outside of the glasses. I held my breath as I swallowed the whiskey down—thanking Parmadale for preparing me to swallow anything.

With frustration, I was learning to bear my lot in life. I managed to accept my role as maid, cook, and wife and silently obeyed Angelo's every whim. He would wake me at all hours of the night and drag me out of bed, demanding for me to make him something to eat. I was relieved on those nights that he only wanted food.

When I realized that our relationship was not a normal father-daughter relationship, Angelo quit telling the story that it was his duty to teach me the facts of life. For a while, he even used a story that God would punish me if I talked about sex to anyone—that nice girls do not talk about sex. When I said I no longer cared what God did to me, Angelo's next maneuver was to remind me that if I ever breathed a word of what was going on in our house, we would both be put in prison, and my brothers would be returned to Parmadale.

Money, cigarettes, and alcohol were my rewards for doing as he pleased with me. When the boys weren't home, I was allowed to sit at the kitchen table with him and have a drink and smoke a cigarette. I only wished he had smoked filtered cigarettes. I never did master not getting the tobacco stuck on my tongue. When the boys were home, Angelo would leave the whiskey or a lit cigarette burning in the ashtray in the bathroom for me. He notified me by nodding his head toward the room. These were the "fun" times. Being his favorite, I was allowed to drink and smoke, and the boys were not. I could get money when he had it just by holding out my hand.

His thinking was incredibly twisted and warped. Angelo had a perverted sense of religious history—like the Adam and Eve story. His version was that it wasn't an apple that got them kicked out of the garden. But rather, Adam got caught eating Eve. He explained that the church couldn't tell the truth to small children and they changed it to an apple.

My own thinking was becoming increasingly cynical. I was trusting life and grownups less as I watched my father charming and conning his way through life.

Despite all the insanity and hardship, I took pride in knowing how to bake bread, cook all the meals, wash clothes in an old-style wringer washing machine, and sew on a manual, foot-pump-operated Singer sewing machine. The only thing I learned about hanging the clothes outside on the clothesline to dry was I hated it. I spent most evenings ironing cotton shirts for Angelo and the boys. Permanent-press was not yet invented.

Mario sometimes did his own shirts, complaining I didn't get the collars pressed even. Albert and Sam could not care less about their appearance and did little to help around the house.

I got so mad at them one morning. I had wanted to bring cupcakes to school the next day for a school fundraiser. Each class was instructed to ask their mothers to help with the bake sale. At times, I tried to hide the fact that we didn't have a mother at home. So I baked. The boys, however, made fun of me for kissing up to the teachers and ate the cupcakes before morning.

Lost in my thoughts, I did what was expected of me. I had no one to turn to, or talk with. The boys, being jealous, had very little to do with me—unless they wanted something from me.

Albert was infuriating. Everyone else got up and ate breakfast at the same time, except for him. He slept in late. When he did stroll out several hours after I had the kitchen cleaned up, he stood in the doorway scratching his head and rubbing his stomach, saying, "Hey Sis, make me something to eat."

One morning I had it with him and screamed out, "Make your own damn breakfast!"

What I didn't know was that Angelo had heard me. He walked in the kitchen and slapped me across the face. I ran from the kitchen and into my room, locking the door behind me.

Angelo screamed to Albert, "Get the ax from the basement! Move your ass, now!"

Albert returned from the basement and handed the ax to Angelo. I lay on the bed, curled up in a ball and leaning against the wall, watching the ax break through the door. Angelo hit the door with the ax until he had ripped a hole big enough to put his arm through. He reached inside and unlocked the door. The door burst open, slamming against the wall as he entered the room.

He stood over me with the ax above my head, "Don't you ever lock that door again!"

He put down his arm, and turned and walked out.

I soon found ways to trick the boys into helping me around the house. "If you don't do this—or if you don't do that—I'll tell dad."

I was losing what little respect I had for myself or others, and I began to lie and steal.

Angelo also taught me the game of shoplifting. There were different rules on different days. On one day, the goal was to see who could steal the most expensive item. On another, we competed to steal the largest one.

After entering a department, grocery, or jewelry store we separated, casually walking up and down the aisles, eyeing the merchandise. First, I found the item I wanted to lift via the "five finger discount." I would then choose a cheap item—worth less than a dollar—and carried both items to the checkout line. With the adrenaline pumping through my veins, I had to focus on staying calm. Waiting in line to pay for this one item, I tucked the other under my coat or put it in my purse.

Angelo thought it was more of an accomplishment to steal big things. His scheme was to pay for the first item, such as a tire for the car. The item was always too big to put in a bag, so the cashier would tag the item with a strip of tape. Angelo rolled the tire out of the store and put it in the trunk of the car. Removing the tape, he ripped it in half and went back into the store and re-tagged two more tires to steal.

For me, stealing came more out of rebellion. Spices for cooking were grossly overpriced. As a way of getting back at the stores, I just lifted them.

I was not allowed out of Angelo's sight. This meant I could only sit on the porch and yell to the girl across the street. If Angelo came out and sat on the porch, I was permitted to ride my bike up and down the street—but not out of his watchful sight. This was because I was a girl, and he loved me, and wanted to protect me. Right!

The boys could go out and stay at the playground each night until nine o'clock. Angelo always instructed them with the same line, delivered slowly and loudly. "If you can't be in this house at nine, then get your asses in this house at one minute to."

My brothers and I fought back at Angelo in the only ways we knew how. Waiting for him to pass out, we sprang into action.

On one occasion, Angelo passed out in the tub while taking a bath. Mario dared me to throw a glass of water at him. I did, but we were all surprised when he didn't react. This time Mario threw it right in his face. Angelo moved only slightly and began mumbling something about the ship—"Get me off this ship."

When we tired of the game, we played cards or watched TV instead. We then went to bed, leaving Angelo in the bathtub.

We all woke to the sound of his voice bellowing through the house as his feet stomped across the wooden floors toward the bedrooms.

"Albert, Mario, Sandy, and Sam—get your asses out here. NOW!"

Angelo's screams brought each of us to our usual lineup position in front of him in the living room. He had put on his pants only. His lips were blue and his feet were bare as he shook his fist at all of us. "What the hell is the matter with you? Why the hell didn't one of you wake me up?"

We knew not to move or even attempt to answer. We stood motionless, staring down at the floor and waited for the lecture to stop and for orders to return to bed.

Mario was growing more ruthless in his pranks. He knew that Angelo walked to the store in the evenings for a pack of cigarettes. On his way home from the playground one day, Mario strung a wire from the base of a tree trunk across the sidewalk and to the fence on the opposite side. I knew Mario was up to something. He was squirming more than usual during dinner. No sooner had dad walked out the door than Mario burst into laughter. He made me and the other two boys promise not to give him away. I wished he had not told me what he had done. It was so hard to keep a straight face when Angelo returned from the store. He stomped up the stairs leading to the porch and slammed the door on his way into the house. His pant leg was torn at the knee.

"Some son-of-a-bitch put a wire across the damn sidewalk!" he screamed.

No one moved. Mario could lie with the best of them and spoke up first, "Oh really. Where was that, dad?"

He got away with it this time, but he wasn't always so successful.

Angelo was very shrewd in hiding his mean-spirited, absolutely maddening-to-deal-with personality. He played people against each other, manipulating them for his self-serving purposes. And it was always the other person who came away feeling guilty or responsible.

To the world outside, Angelo had a magnetism about him that sucked people into believing his cons—from getting out of well-deserved driving tickets, to getting store credit for booze, food and clothing. He conned his way everywhere he went.

I was in the seventh grade now, and anybody who was anybody had a leather coat. When I asked for one, he walked me into Wilson Leather Coats in Cleveland. Sitting there, I watched him con the store manager with one of his tales of woe about how he just couldn't send his little girl to school anymore without a coat. Angelo went on to tell him about how he was raising four children all alone since their mother ran off. The manager questioned him, "Why a leather coat?" and Angelo replied, "Wouldn't you want your children to have the best?"

I proudly walked out of the store, perfumed in the rich smell of leather.

At one time Angelo worked in the maintenance department at a local TV station. He made friends with the guy who played the host on a children's show.

Angelo would often sneak off to a local bar during his shift and watch the show from his stool. Part of the show was a skit with an empty cage where his friend would visit with the Invisible Butterfly. He would alert Angelo that the bosses were looking for him by strolling over to the cage and saying, "Now, boys and girls, let's see where the Invisible Butterfly is." Angelo knew this was his clue to get back to the station.

Women stared or flirted with him as he passed them on the street or at the corner store, and Angelo was glad to reciprocate. Embarrassed by the attention they paid him, I sometimes tried to discourage Angelo by saying, "Yeah, but she's married."

They never heard his mumbled replies. "So what. That doesn't plug up the hole."

On a rare family outing, Angelo took us swimming at a local park, and our neighbors trusted him to take their two children with us. Albert, now fifteen, got permission to follow us there in a separate car with his two friends, one of whom was now sixteen and driving his own car.

Everyone else ran off to go swimming as soon as we arrived. I stayed behind and set up the picnic area. Relieved to be out of the house and doing anything different, I refused to be angry when, once again, I was left to take care of everything while the boys ran off to play. Angelo lay down on the blanket next to the picnic table as I put the hamburgers on the grill.

When the food was ready, I went and called the boys over to eat. Angelo had dozed off to sleep. I nudged him a few times. "Dad, your cheeseburger is ready."

Finally, he stirred. Sitting up slowly, he reached for the cheeseburger. For a moment he just sat there. The boys and their friends sat at the table and watched Angelo's slow movements in shock and disbelief. I was embarrassed. This was the first time I remember anyone outside the family seeing my father loaded on pills, and how unpredictable his behavior could be. He opened his mouth and sank his teeth into the bun, then stopped. We waited for him to continue. He didn't. He passed out face down, still holding the cheeseburger between his teeth. Angrily, I went over to him and pulled the cheeseburger from his face—then threw it as far as I could. I pushed him over and Angelo lay on his side for hours.

The sun had been down for at least an hour, and we were the last people hanging around the park. It was getting dark and the other kids who came with us were starting to worry and complain that their parents would be mad if we didn't get them home soon.

I had been trying to wake Angelo for over a half hour. When he finally came to the first thing out of his mouth was, "Where's my cheeseburger?"

Slurring his words, he repeated, "Where's my cheeeeseburrrrrger?"

"You ate it already," I barked, urging him to get up. "We have to get the neighbor kids home!"

With Mario on one side and me on the other, we managed to get Angelo to his feet. As we walked toward the parking lot, Angelo looked down and, before we could stop him, he bent over to pick up the cheeseburger that had been on the ground and out in the sun all afternoon. "You're not going to eat that?" I cried out as I tried to grab it from him.

"A little dirt never hurt anybody," he said as he took a bite.

We got him to the car and dumped him in the driver's seat. He took minutes trying to get the keys out of his pocket—and minutes longer staring into his opened hand, trying to find the car key mixed in with his change. Losing all patience with him, I proceeded to assist him by pulling the key from his hand and putting it in the ignition. I started the car from the passenger seat.

We drove around and around the parking lot, circling each time past the exit. Albert and his friends followed behind us, driving at two or three miles per hour before stopping. They laughed, thinking this scene was hilarious. One of Albert's friends came up with an idea. He got out of his car and, on foot, walked up to our car, making loud imitation siren sounds repeatedly. In a deep voice, he yelled into Angelo's opened window, "PULL OVER. THIS IS THE POLICE."

Angelo was too stoned to realize what was really going on and stopped the car. It wouldn't have been the first time Angelo had been pulled over for drunk driving. Never looking up, he automatically reached for his driver's license. After exchanging a few words, Angelo agreed with the pretend cop to move over, and he let the boy drive us home.

The boys went out to play every night after dinner. My father, however, informed me "Nice girls don't run around on playgrounds, hanging around with boys."

I hated being a girl.

71

Everything I wanted to do was rejected: "No, you can't do this," or "You can't do that!"; "Because you're a girl!"

I did have a way of getting even with or torturing my brothers, all in the name of having a good time. Albert and Sam shared a double bed. Early in the mornings, I would sneak into the room while they were sleeping and hide behind the double bed. The bed was just far enough away from the wall for me to stand behind the headboard. I leaned over it and dangled a long string down and across the chest of one of them until he woke. This was always enough to provoke one into punching the other, crying out, "Cut it out!" Each believed it was the other who was playing games.

Mario, however, did catch me on occasion and got in on the fun—the fun of torturing me. He waited for me to make my "getaway," and as I was about to exit the room Mario proceeded to throw a shoe from his bed across the room, hitting me in the back. This caused me to scream out in pain, waking Albert and Sam.

Albert tried hard to live up to some idea that he was the oldest of the four and, therefore, responsible for us. He was certainly a dreamer. "One day I'm going to be a baseball player," he said, or "I'm going to be a psychologist when I grow up."

He also had a habit of rocking his head back and forth till he dropped off to sleep. When he wasn't sleeping, he was listening to baseball on his hand-held transistor radio pressed to his ear, while at the same time watching the game on TV. When he did go outside, he was always playing softball.

Then, Albert started taking the pills that he stole from dad.

Mario could make me laugh; he never seemed to take anything seriously. He could be funny, and he could also be mean with the practical jokes. Hiding under a table, waiting for me to pass by, he would leap up to scare the hell out of me. He did anything for attention, and Sam and I were the ones who were available at home.

Another favorite pastime for Mario was to catch mice in the house and, opening my bedroom door, dangle them by their tails. After I screamed, he would throw them at me. Without the scream, it wasn't any fun for Mario.

mario -funny brother.

72

He was always chasing or being chased by the girls. His black hair was combed and slicked back. He took great pride in his appearance. He spent more time than I ever did on combing and putting every hair in place. Mario could have passed for Alfalfa in the mornings. He hated it when I called him this. One day, he took a swing at a teacher in study hall just for messing up his hair.

Yearning for attention, he spent most of his time lying on the ground or hiding in the bushes, making out with the twelve-year-old girl in the neighborhood; or he would sneak a girl home to hide in the basement.

He never figured out how I caught him each time. He didn't know I could hear the girl's pleas from the floor register in my bedroom, "No, Mario, we shouldn't." But the heavy breathing only stopped after I went into the kitchen and called out, "Mario, is that you? Are you home?"

He flew up the stairs, "What do you want?"

Smirking at him, I replied, "Nothing. I was just wondering if you were home."

"Yeah, I'm home. So what? Keep your mouth shut or you'll wake the old man," he responded.

"What are you doing down there, Mario?" I pushed on.

Frustrated with my interruptions he replied hastily. "Nothing. I'm getting my clothes ready for school."

I gradually watched Mario withdraw from laughter as he became filled with bitterness and anger. Angelo yelled, screamed, and punched on Mario the most. Before he was eleven or twelve years old, I witnessed him recoil in anger one day. Tight-fisted, and with his arms tensed at his sides, he locked his jaw to take the blows as Angelo's fist punched him in the face.

"Go ahead and hit me, you bastard, if it makes you feel like a man," he screamed.

Mario never shed a tear. Angelo took another swing. I tried to stop Mario from egging Angelo on, and cried out for Angelo to please stop hitting him.

Mario became accustomed to being Angelo's human punching bag, and never showed fear from then on. He started getting involved in bigger and bigger pranks, which led to stealing cars and crossing the state border in a stolen vehicle. At thirteen years old, he was sentenced in juvenile court to serve time in a boys' home.

Sam, on the other hand, didn't seem to care for, or notice, girls. He was now eleven, and was possibly the most normal or least affected of the children at the time. He showed little interest in contact sports. Gambling became his favorite pastime—not to mention the money he won. At the age of eleven, Sam was playing cards and winning money away from the older boys who hung around on the playground. This was not without its dangers. The fourteen- to seventeen-year-olds who played cards or shot craps did not take kindly to losing their money to a kid Sam's age. And there was always the fear of the cops sneaking up on them after waiting for the pot to build up to twenty or thirty dollars. They would step in, take the pot, and tell the kids to get on home or they would haul them in for illegal gambling. When Sam spotted them coming, he would grab the money, jump on his bike, and pedal as fast as his legs could go to get away and home before the cops could catch him.

Sam was not too elated when I reached out my hand, demanding half of the money. Threatening to report him to dad, I held him hostage for the money, which was later used to buy food.

Angelo didn't need a reason to give us a beating.

Sam returned home one evening and found me crying as he walked through the front door. "What are you crying about? He never hits you."

I moved my hand from my face before responding to Sam's criticism.

Exposing my now blackened eye—I replied "Oh really!"

Sam bolted back toward the door as Angelo leaned around the corner from the wall between the living room and dining room. "Sam, get your ass over here," Angelo yelled.

Sam moved cautiously towards Angelo. Angelo leaped up from his chair and slapped him upside the head. Sam left the room and went to bed without looking back.

As I got older—all of thirteen—I was throwing temper tantrums and running to my bedroom often. The boys just laughed at me.

When I realized I could sit there all night without them caring or looking for me, I began pushing the dresser in front of the door and waited by the open window for the boys to leave after supper.

Angelo's visits to my room stopped once I began my monthly menstruation cycles. So, with Angelo passing out soon after dinner each night, I began climbing out the window and followed closely behind Albert, Mario, and Sam—following them to the playground. I hid behind trees, cars, or in the bushes, waiting to see what they were doing. They never could figure out which one of their friends kept me informed of their doings. If I later needed them to help me around the house or wanted money, I reminded them, "If you don't . . . I'll tell dad about. . . ."

Her first boyfriend

I started dating the guy next door, referred to by most at school as "Killer." He was sixteen and owned a car. "Killer" became my self-appointed body guard after I was beaten up at school by a group of black kids.

I gave up following my brothers around. Accepting the fact that I was a girl and to them the enemy, I learned to keep more to myself—always pretending to be much older and tougher than them.

Inside, I was scared to death and wondered what I was becoming. I was now sneaking out the window to go out with my boyfriend and another couple. We usually went to a drive-in where we drank beer and made out. It didn't take long for the alcohol to take effect. But Killer never pushed me to go any further than French kissing or "dry humping" with our clothes on.

The charm of having a boyfriend, being "Killer's girlfriend," ran its course and now I was worried sick. How was I going to break up with this guy? I finally reached for the telephone and called him. He did not take the news well. I knew the street way of keeping your reputation or image meant he would make it look as if, or tell others, that he dumped me. But I was not prepared for him to have his sister beat me up that afternoon. Later, while drinking and driving, he drove his car into a telephone pole—killing himself instantly at the age of sixteen.

Killer dies @ 16 after Sandy breaks up w/ him.

Albert, Mario, and Sam always acted as if my life was charmed because I was a girl—my life was anything but charmed. I had to fight for anything I got, just as everybody else did.

Angelo did not send me to California to live with Tony because I was special. He sent me to California to save his own ass. When the police were called in by a suspecting neighbor, I was the one who was taken away in the police car—taken to a nearby hospital and laid out on a table with my legs up in stirrups. With no explanation as to what was happening to me, two female police officers stood by while the cold steel was inserted into my body parts. A doctor came in and tried to calm me by saying, "It's going to be all right. I just need to check you." This was the same line dad had used on me. I went into hysteria, screaming and trying to bolt off the table: "this doctor is not checking me." It took the strength of the two policewomen and two nurses to hold me down for the examination. Angelo's uncanny luck—no sperm was found.

I was so humiliated and scared to death after all Dad's warnings about my going to prison and the boys returning to the orphanage. The boys would all hate me because it would have been my fault.

Dad was not willing to take any chances. So, within a week or two he planned to send me to Tony's to get rid of the evidence (me). He had made all the arrangements with Tony, telling him that I was getting older and wilder—that he wanted me to get out of Cleveland. I came home from school one day. Angelo had my suitcase packed and notified me, "You're going to California." Before I could speak a word, the cab arrived. Angelo and my brothers escorted me to the airport.

We all wanted to know why was I going to California. "Why can't the boys come with me?" I asked, seeing the look of disappointment in their faces. Instead of getting an answer from him, the boys did what they always seemed to do—make a joke out of it. "Because she's a girl."

So, we sat together one last time, the four of us kids huddled together at the airport restaurant, drinking soda pop and eating potato chips. This was the last meal we shared together.

Angelo, of course, sat and had a few drinks while flirting with the waitresses. When we got up to leave he played the big shot, throwing down a few bills for a tip. The boys on the other hand, never missing a chance to pick up a few bucks, proceeded to rip off the tip. They walked me to the gate for departure.

Chapter Seven—Captive

I HAD FIVE HOURS ON THE PLANE to try and remember all I could about Tony and Becky. I had only met Becky once, just before they got married. She was small in size and not any taller than me. Unlike me, she carried all her weight high in the front. She had a strong accent, having been born and raised in Kentucky. Shortly after graduation from high school, innocent and excited about moving to the big city, she and a girlfriend drove to Cleveland.

That is where she met Tony, and after a three or four week courtship the justice of the peace married them. Tony was on the rebound from a relationship that ended when he left his fiancée standing at the altar.

He had succeeded in getting out of Cleveland and had moved to California, where he went to work as a dispatcher for the railroads, and Becky found employment as a factory worker. They purchased a home in La Mirada with a VA loan.

I had only seen Tony a handful of times in my life, since we had been raised in different households. He got angry with me once for introducing him as my half-brother.

He claimed that he did come to visit me and the boys in Parmadale while home on leave from the army. I only remember his coming into Cleveland unannounced and stirring up trouble for me.

Shrugging my shoulders, I excused the whole episode as him wanting to believe he was only acting on my behalf. I also knew I couldn't hold this against him if I wanted the opportunity to live in California.

The anticipation of what life now held in store for me kept my mind racing. Seated at the front of the airplane, with legs crossed at the ankles, I fought to keep still. I wanted to jump out of the seat and pace up and down the aisle. I tried not to look out of the window next to me for fear of throwing up. The airline stewardess came by again. Smiling much too often, she repeated her overused line, "Honey, can I bring anything?"

Angered by her demeanor, I replied as politely as I could, "No, thank you."

I wished she would stop speaking to me as though I were a small child. I was almost fourteen years old. Standing five feet, four inches tall and weighing ninety-eight pounds, I wore no makeup and had long, stringy, dark brown hair that was parted down the middle. I was dressed in a knee-length, black leather coat buttoned all the way down.

My teeth were always such an embarrassment to me. One of my front teeth was twisted almost sideways, and another was bucked outward. I rarely smiled. Mario tortured me, calling me "Bucky Beaver" and many other assorted names. I never smiled without first holding my hand up in front of my mouth so others would not see how crooked my teeth were. Most people guessed my age to be about eleven or twelve years.

The lights flashed for all passengers to return to their seats and fasten their seat belts. I tried pushing the thought of being sick out of my mind by taking deep breaths until the plane was on the ground. This was my first flight, and I was not happy with the takeoff or landing. For a few moments my thoughts were on the landing, not on arriving in California.

Once on the ground, the stewardess tried to take my hand and walk me off the plane. Was she nuts? Did she think I would permit her to embarrass me, just because my father had instructed her to do so? I pulled my hand back and walked beside her, carrying one small suitcase with everything I owned in it. I was terrified as I stood in the terminal, wondering if Tony would really be there to pick me up. I didn't notice him until he turned to face me.

Tony pranced around the terminal as if he were a small child waiting for a parade. He was taller than me, but he was certainly not more than five foot seven. Yet he carried himself with self-assured conceit. Tony had one hand tucked inside his pocket, smoking a cigarette with the other. His black hair was no longer the clean-cut, military style. Now, it hung down past his ears and covered the back of his neck. He was dressed in Levi's and a t-shirt, and was much skinnier than I remembered. Grinning as he motioned me to him, Tony was anxious and proud to have someone to show off for.

"Look Becky, there's my sister!"

Becky greeted me coyly, having just as many doubts as I did about my moving in with them. Tony had persuaded Becky that I would be very helpful to her around the house. Of course, Tony stood to gain as well. His moving to California and buying a home at age twenty-one was not enough for his ego. He needed attention and constant approval from someone other than his wife.

Tony led the way through the airport and out to the car. I remembered something else about the Cicero men—they all had the annoying habit of pacing themselves well ahead of the women they were with, leaving the women racing to keep up.

Tony talked nonstop as we drove from LAX to La Mirada. His excitement and energy were infectious. I was confused, but hopeful that this just might be my "great white hope." Living in California with my big brother was the break I had been waiting for.

My eyes widened as we drove through the neighborhood. All the houses were lined up perfectly on manicured lawns. We pulled into the driveway of their single-story ranch house. Tony, jerking us all forward with the sudden stopping of the car, jumped out and walked quickly ahead. Opening the front door to the house, he stood back to call out "Come on, Sandy."

I looked at Becky, wondering how she was taking all this.

"You'd better git goinn. Yurrr brotherrr is waitinn fer youuu," she said.

Just inside the front door, we were greeted by a small white poodle. "This is Kilo," Tony announced as he raced me through for the grand tour of his house. In each area, in and out of the house, he pointed out every detail along the way. He boasted as he pointed toward the swimming pool in the backyard, "Look, I have a swimming pool" —as though I couldn't see it.

Continuing on, we went back inside the sliding glass doors to the kitchen and living room, which was complete with a pool table—then down the hall to what was to be my bedroom, across the hall from theirs. Becky left with the dog and disappeared into her bedroom. The third bedroom was converted into a den, and was complete with a reel-to-reel tape player and brightly colored plastic strings of beads hanging in the doorway. The house was furnished throughout in contemporary furniture recently purchased from Sears.

Tony was disappointed and wasted no time in letting me know that I was not showing him the praise and excitement he had been craving. I told him how nice I thought the house was.

"Nice!" he screamed.

"Twenty-five thousand dollars for this house and all you can say is nice!"

I apologized quickly, "Yes, this is great Tony."

My enthusiasm was lacking. I had lived in far too many situations to get excited, and knew my days here would also be numbered.

The following morning was Saturday, and we had the weekend to get acquainted. Tony and Becky were eager to take me sightseeing, and we spent the day at Disneyland.

On Sunday, they took me to their favorite store, Sears, to shop for school clothes. I was to start yet another new school on Monday—but I wasn't going to let that spoil my first weekend in California. I was in awe of Southern California. Just driving around, everything looked so bright and new. Buildings were massive. The homes were incredible in size and design. This was unlike anything I could have ever imagined, coming from Ohio.

Yet, pretending that it was no big deal, I didn't allow myself to show these new emotions. I kept flipping in and out of fear—fear of having to go back to Cleveland gripped me. I had heard the message my whole life, "If you don't be good," "If you don't behave, you're going back to . . . "

Becky drove me to school on Monday morning. I wore one of the new dresses she had picked out for me. I hated the dress but kept quiet, not wanting to hurt Becky's feelings. But this dress was ugly. It was dark brown with a floral print covering it. I kept myself hidden under the black, knee-length leather coat, even though it was seventy degrees outside.

I'd rather sweat than be seen in this dress. I was dreading going to the new school again.

The school was enormous and spread out over several acres. It had rows and rows of modern prefab structures with trees, shrubs, and flowers planted everywhere. This was in stark contrast to the school I had just left in Cleveland, which was more than fifty years old—a three-story brick building, standing alone on a busy neighborhood street.

The style of dress in La Mirada had already changed to extremely casual—Levi's, sandals, tie-dyed shirts, and long hair. No one else was wearing a bland dark dress or a black leather coat. It was February in California and the sun was shining. I was sweating, but not about to remove the coat.

I was uneasy all morning and during the break, watching all the other kids in school. I had never seen so many people gathered together in one place, seemingly having fun—I was curious about them because they seemed so casual and friendly with each other.

I felt awkward and stood alone. The other girls my age were huddled together, giggling and laughing. These kids spent freely at the school snack bar, not at all concerned about where their next meal or money would come from. We certainly didn't have this kind of luxury where I just came from.

School in Cleveland was very different. For one, we didn't walk around smiling. We spent our time watching out for the school bullies, hoping not to get caught up in a fight. I trusted no one, and rarely let my guard down.

When one of the girls approached, she smiled and nodded toward the leather coat, "What a bitchin' coat."

I responded, "Oh, really!"

The girl, unaware she had offended me, repeated herself, "What a bitchin' coat."

With that, I unbuttoned the coat and handed it to the girl standing next to her. Moving in closer to my target, I replied, "Oh yeah, you like my coat?" and proceeded to punch her in the face. To my surprise, she burst into tears and turned to run away from me.

Now I was really confused. I didn't hit her that hard.

Kids gathered around, trying to see what had happened. It left me baffled. Why didn't she want to fight? A teacher came up to the scene and asked me to please follow him to the principal's office. Once in the office, I was questioned as to why I would do such a cruel thing to someone. Having no respect for authority and knowing they wouldn't understand or care anyway, I didn't respond to their questioning.

Tony was angry to be called into the principal's office on my first day in school. "I hope you don't think you're going to get away with this kind of crap and live with me!"

On the way back to the house I tried to explain to him that the girl was making fun of my coat, and when she called me a bitch, that's when I let her have it.

Tony's response was a slap in the face. "You idiot! She didn't call you a bitch. She said your coat was bitchin'. And here in California that means she liked your coat."

Life, once again, had changed, and this time the language changed with it. The kids made fun of me for saying things differently, such as "Let's go by . . .'s house after school."

"Why, is it for sale?" they laughed.

Unnerved, this prompted me not to ask any questions and to say very little for fear others would find out how stupid I was. Some of my problems came from not understanding the slang, others from my lack of formal education.

The next day in school, I was greeted by a boy named Tom, who came to meet me during the break. Having heard about the fight the day before, he was amused by the story of the new girl in school and invited me to the parking lot to smoke some "weed."

I agreed to follow him, thinking he was referring to a cigarette. Several others were already in the parking lot.

Another thing I noticed immediately was that these kids had cars in the parking lot to go out to during school breaks, and they listened to music while hanging around smoking and talking about the upcoming party or concert. The only kids I knew back home with cars had them only for a few hours—they were stolen.

I watched silently as Tom lit the joint, wondering to myself why these kids were all sharing a cigarette. High-class Californians and they have to share a cigarette? "Here, try one of mine," I said, as I pulled a pack of Marlboros from my purse.

The group burst out laughing. "Go ahead and try this one, Sandy," Tom said as he handed me the joint.

I took the joint, then started inhaling and releasing the smoke as with any cigarette.

"No, like this!"

Tom corrected me as he put the joint between his lips. He inhaled the smoke, holding it in for a long time before releasing it. I tried to do as he instructed, only to find myself choking. They all began laughing and looking at each other, realizing I didn't know we were smoking pot.

Tom invited me to his house after school for a party. His parents were out of town and had left him home alone. The house filled up with about twenty-five kids from the school—all smoking pot, drinking beer and wine. Guys took off their clothes down to their boxer shorts while a couple of girls stripped to bras and underpants to go swimming. I sat alone watching.

Many new experiences were surrounding me. These people were so laid back and didn't seem to have a care in the world—they talked of the latest music or newest band that was out, or what concert they were going to that weekend.

The pot was beginning to take effect. My head was getting lighter and I felt calm for the first time. Giving in to the mood, I allowed myself to relax onto the floor facing upward. I stared at the ceiling while listening to music play on the stereo. Alcohol had made me feel superior and stronger, while pot allowed me to be at ease and put a smile on my face. Now for the first time since arriving in California, I didn't worry much about anything—maybe the first time in my life. I liked this drug. I even considered giving up booze—this stuff was good. The only problem was it did make me thirsty. So I followed it with a glass of wine. If you can call Spinada with a screw top cap wine. This was the wine brand of choice with my new friends. Not too many of them were into the hard liquor my friends and I drank in Cleveland. Everyone in California seemed to be drinking wine or beer.

In my family, beer is considered a breakfast beverage—and works much better than aspirin for hangovers.

Hiding my drug use from Tony and Becky was proving to be a challenge. Tony and Becky were the enemy and not to be trusted. I smiled when I had to and did as I was told, waiting for the moment when I could get out of the house and run to my newfound friends, but more importantly the drugs.

I was now getting stoned on a daily basis. Money wasn't a problem. A joint cost fifty cents and speed was going for a buck. I used my lunch allowance to buy all the pot or pills I needed to get through the days.

Tony and Becky did not have the picture-perfect marriage they portrayed at first. Tony was gone most of the time, claiming to be working. We later found out he was cheating on her every chance he could. She was ignorant of what he was up to, or at least put on a pretty good show of not noticing.

Becky worked long hours as a factory worker and made it clear to me that the chores around the house were now mine. The payoff was always the same from Becky. In the sweet-talking and child-like tones of her Kentucky drawl, she would coax me, "Sandy, if you do such and such I'll give you a cigarette."

Cleaning the house or cooking her dinner was worth four cigarettes. Watching her favorite television shows with her was another two cigarettes. When not working, Becky slept. On her days off, she enjoyed lying in bed with the dog and eating popcorn. The real thrill came from watching Tom Jones or Roller Derby—both of which I detested. At fifteen years old, when all my friends and I were listening to groups like The Beatles, I had a tough time putting up with her choices. I also didn't obey her for the cigarettes. I was already buying my own cigarettes and pot, but I did it to keep the peace in the house.

Becky was naive. Tony was quick to point this out to me if I missed seeing something dumb or foolish she had done. Tony, like my parents, played people against each other. Becky and I were no different. In front of Becky, Tony conned me into cooking for him, knowing she would get mad because he asked me and not her. He also made fun of her speech. "Honneee, wooould youuu go to the marr-kett and git meee ssomme mmilk. Youu cann git a feeww dollarrs outta my billfold over there in my pocketbooook."

Becky did pull a few stunts that made me wonder about her. The house was cold one evening. Becky decided that if it was necessary for her to turn up the heat in the house, the fish in the aquarium must have been cold as well. So she cranked the heat up on the aquarium. I thought Tony was going to kill her when he noticed the "fish fry." All the fish were floating on the top of the water.

Another time, Becky had turned the water on to take a bath. While waiting for the tub to fill up, she had drifted off to sleep. When Tony came into the house that night he went into one of his many rages, screaming about the water that now soaked through the carpets.

Tony terrorized Becky with his "suck the life" out of you intensity. I was humiliated, scared, and embarrassed for Becky when he went into one of his bouts of screaming obscenities and insults at her. He dominated the relationship with her, me, and anyone he befriended. Anyone unfortunate enough to be Tony's "friend" would have to endure his intense anger, which on many occasions led to physical harm.

Tony and Becky frequently reminded me how lucky I was to be living not only in California, but with them in a house with a pool.

I couldn't turn to Becky for advice or help because I had no respect for her. She acted with little girl innocence in front of Tony or others, yet displayed a split personality with me. One minute she could be warm and friendly, and the next minute she snapped with agitation. They both played watchdog over me, putting down and making fun of my friends. Becky was careful with her remarks. Tony, however, made his rude remarks out loud for all to hear. Not caring if his behavior made me or anyone around him uncomfortable, he thrived on threatening looks and insulting others. I learned to sneak in and out of the house whenever I wanted to get away, or get loaded— most often both.

Gracie Rogers and I met in school. We sat next to each other in class at the back of the room, and quickly developed a liking for one another. Gracie was very pretty and had long, blonde hair and freckles all over. She was somewhat shy at first—but laughed at all my bantering about the class or the teacher. I encouraged her to meet with Tom and the rest of the gang. We became somewhat inseparable from that day on and were happy that we lived only a few streets away from each other. We began walking to and from school. I stopped by her house to pick her up each day.

The first time I went to her house to get her, I was surprised when she opened the door and stood there smiling at me. I wasn't sure what to make of her sudden change in clothing style. Like me, she usually dressed in faded Levi's with holes torn in the knees, long straight hair parted down the middle, and no makeup. But now, she stood before me dressed in pink baby doll shoes and a pink dress, her hair curled, and she was wearing makeup. Even though she looked great, I wasn't about to say so. I was disappointed she didn't tell me that she was planning to dress up—not that I would have followed. I didn't even own lipstick. I hated the way my mother looked, with her lips and nails painted red. And I never got into makeup when the other girls my age did.

"Are you coming in?" she questioned, eyeing me as though I was the one who was dressed differently.

"No, I think we should be on our way to school," I snapped. Looking away from her piercing eyes, I was annoyed and hurt she didn't offer any explanation as to why she was dressed this way for school.

Just then, Gracie's voice came from behind the girl who was standing in the doorway. I realized this was not Gracie grinning at me. It was her identical twin sister, Tiffany, who enjoyed playing tricks on anyone who would fall for her pranks—including some of Gracie's dates. Most people could only tell them apart by the way they dressed.

.

We had another school friend, Linda Jaramillo, who lived two doors away from the Rogers'. Linda's mother and I did not get along. She thought I was a bad influence on her daughter and did not want me hanging around with her. Little did her mother know that it was her darling son, Paul, who was supplying his sister, Tom, and me with drugs. Linda and Paul's bedrooms were located in the front of the house. She and I devised a system for me to see her. We hung a string outside her bedroom window with a bell tied to one end, and I would ring the bell for Linda to let me climb in through the window. When we heard her mother coming down the hallway, I hid in the closet until she was gone.

It was fun having friends to pal around with. Other than my short relationship with Jeri Bain in Cleveland, this was the first time I had friends. And when we didn't want to go to school we went to the beach, the movies, or simply hung out together.

Things just happened for me; I gave little thought of what outcome my actions would bring to me or my friends.

I borrowed a car from Linda's brother Paul one day, promising him that I would share some of the drugs I was picking up elsewhere. While driving back to Paul's, I saw Gracie and Tiffany walking along the sidewalk. I stopped to pick them up. The car was filled with all kinds of excitement and noise. The girls couldn't believe I had talked Paul into letting me drive his car. The pills I had taken were now affecting my vision and judgment. In my attempt to stop for a red light, the car slammed into another car in the middle of the intersection. I panicked and yelled to the others, "Get out and run!"

Tiffany protested, "What are you doing?"

"If you don't want to go to jail, you'd better run," I commanded.

Paul had instructed me that if anything happened he would report the car stolen. So, with that I grabbed the keys from the ignition and we all ran down a residential street and past people who were out walking their dogs. I could not believe it when some of the people who had seen the accident started to chase after us.

Growing exhausted, I knew I couldn't run much more and stopped. Finding a row of bushes in front of a house that was a few blocks from the accident, I whispered instructions for the girls to jump behind them and hide. Gracie and I did. Tiffany didn't and was caught by the police a block from where we had stopped.

Gracie and I stayed down and hidden behind the shrubs for over an hour while the neighbors gathered to see what all the noise and commotion was. The overhead noise from the police helicopter alerted them that something was going on. Gracie was freaking— crying and begging me to get her home. I listened carefully to every sound around us, amazed to hear one woman telling another that she saw a "guy" jump out of the driver's side, and two other kids or girls running away from the vehicle.

When all the people had given up the search and the police stopped circling the area, I knew we had to take our chances and start home. We proceeded slowly from the bushes. I had to keep reminding Gracie to slow down. "If you walk too fast, we will look suspicious."

We made it home safely—I thought. Lying in bed when the doorbell rang, I stiffened and listened to Mr. Rogers explain to Becky that his daughter was in jail for stealing a car; she didn't know how to drive, and he was sure that Sandy was involved.

Becky called me to the front door. When I pretended not to know what was going on, Mr. Rogers informed me that either I could go to the station with him or he would send the police to my door. Becky agreed to follow him to the station, and she complained all the way there about all the trouble I was in.

After being questioned by the police officer, I was charged with stealing a car, hit-and-run for literally running on foot, leaving the scene of an accident, and for being under the influence of narcotics. The officer explained that since I had turned myself in and had cooperated, I could be released to go home that night but would be required to report back for a juvenile court hearing.

The charges were dropped because of my age, and at fifteen years old I did get a restriction stating I could not get a driver's license in California until I was eighteen. Tony and Becky also put me on restriction for a month.

This did not turn out to be so bad after all. I had become somewhat of a celebrity at school. The story of my weekend excursion got around. Ironically, the passenger in the car I hit was also a student at La Mirada High. When I passed him on campus after the accident, he always smiled at me and remarked, "Hey, didn't I run into you somewhere before?"

Once Tony and Becky left to work their swing-shift jobs, I had parties at the house. The word was out that "Cicero" was having a party and the house would fill with fifty to one hundred kids from school. There was no way for me to control the numbers. This went on for months.

One morning after a party, Tony waltzed into my bedroom and instructed me, "Get packed. We're going to Cleveland."

In my hung over state, I thought they were finally returning me to Cleveland as punishment. I did not protest and packed the small beige suitcase I had arrived with. We drove nonstop to Cleveland in three days, thanks to the convenience of "little white crosses," also known as "speed." Tony and Becky, however, did not see this as taking drugs. Their "white crosses" were for medicinal purposes—the kind of medication they needed to work, or for driving.

I vaguely remembered about the telephone call from Aunt Laura the night before. She was brief and to the point: "Your brother, Albert, is dead. His helicopter was shot down in Nam. This is long distance, so I can't stay on the phone."

Tony decided to detour through Kentucky and took us to the boys' home where Mario had been for over a year—now serving a sentence for car theft. Tony, somehow, was able to convince the authorities of the juvenile facility to release Mario into his custody after explaining Albert's death, and we brought Mario back to Cleveland with us for Albert's funeral.

After racing from Los Angeles to Cleveland, Aunt Laura revealed the truth. "Your no-good father was loaded on those damn pills of his, and he made the story up. Albert is not dead." We learned he had made up the whole story after receiving documents from the army indicating Albert had been shipped overseas. Somehow, my father's mind had twisted this into "Your son's body is being shipped overseas."

We had just driven three thousand miles, grieving the loss of a brother—only to find out it was a fabrication of my father's drugged mind.

Tony quickly went into a rage and raced out of the house to search for Angelo. He found him in a bar. Grabbing hold of Angelo's shoulder, he swung him around to face him. As he swore at him, Tony's arm started forward but was stopped by someone from behind who prevented him from landing his fist onto Angelo's face.

We only stayed in town one day. Mario went to live with Angelo and Sam in a dingy east side apartment. Tony, Becky, and I headed back to California. I accepted my school friends' sympathy and continued to lie to them about my brother's death. How could I possibly explain to them that my father made it up?

Home life was becoming more of a challenge, as I tried to live up to Tony and Becky's expectations of me. Tony wanted me to be amused by his constant verbal assaults on his wife. Becky demanded that I do all the cooking, cleaning, and laundry around the house. She made me livid by constantly changing her mind, telling me I could do something one minute and then preventing me from doing it when the time arrived.

Tony was now in lust over some "chick" he met at the local bar. Always looking to impress me, he instructed me to watch while he told Becky he needed to get away for a few days "to find himself."

Becky did not question him and even packed his bag. Tony left for the weekend. I just shook my head in disbelief. How could anyone be that gullible?

I was looking forward to going to Knotts Berry Farm with Gracie and the gang that Friday night. Becky had told me earlier that morning that I could go if all of my chores were done when she got home. When she came home from work, I served her dinner and, while I cleaned up her dishes, she lit up a cigarette and told me I had to stay in.

"But you said!" I protested.

"Don't matterr whad I said beferr, yoo're staayinn in the house," she snapped back.

I turned away from her and faced toward the sink, hiding my anger inside, and finished with the dishes. Becky left the room and had gone into her bedroom to lie down. I went in the living room and turned on the TV. She came stomping down the hall, into the room and turned off the TV. "I'm tryinn tooo git some sleep."

Going into my room, I closed the door, turned the radio on softly, and lay down on my bed. Again, Becky barged through the door and screamed, "I TOILED YOOUU I doonnn't wannn nooisse in thees howsse."

I waited over an hour before she finally fell asleep. Sneaking around quietly, I wrote a brief note: "Becky, I went out! Why? Because I felt like it!"—then escaped the house.

By the time I had arrived at Gracie's, the gang had gone on without me. I fought back any tears and, instead, cursed Tony and Becky. I hated living with them, but I knew I had very few options. So I walked to the corner liquor store and waited outside for someone to buy me a bottle of wine. Returning to the Rogers' house, I proceeded to drink alone in the camper that they kept parked in the driveway. Escaping via the bottle was my answer. I passed out, not waking until morning.

Hung over, I walked home with my head pounding—stopping along the way to throw up. I didn't expect Becky to be home when I got back to the house. I had intentionally planned to return after she should have left for work.

She didn't go to work that morning. Instead, she waited for me and took the opportunity to jump me from behind as I came out of the bathroom and was walking toward my bedroom. I had dry heaves after throwing up all the way home. This was the first time I had experienced all the symptoms of vomiting, with my stomach tightening and contracting, but nothing coming up. I wanted to die. Becky's sudden appearance was not welcomed. She leaped up onto my back like a monkey. Her arms gripped firmly around my neck, and she wrapped her legs around my body while she screamed into my ear, "So, the little whore is home!"

At this moment, I didn't care or even think about my actions. I tried pulling her off of me, but she kept coming back, leaping onto my shoulders as I tried to get away from her. I began slamming her repeatedly backwards into the wall. Becky screamed out mockingly, "Wait till your brother gits home. You're going back to Cleveland."

I let it all out and began screaming at her. "I don't care! You are so stupid! Do you really believe the story your husband told you? You're the idiot around here! My brother is not writing any damn book up in the mountains, he's screwing some chick he picked up last week at the bar."

Becky stood still for a moment before releasing me. Finally, she left me alone to sleep off my hangover. We didn't see or speak to each other again all day.

The vibration of the garage door opening startled me. Becky ran from the bedroom when she heard Tony's car pull in the garage. She greeted him at the door by throwing a lamp at him as he entered the house. This triggered one of the worst fights I witnessed between the two of them. Tony wasted no time trying to figure out what was going on and jumped right in, slamming Becky to the floor. He pounced on top of her and slapped her in the face. "What the hell's the matter with you?"

Becky responded by grabbing hold of an ashtray and hit him in the head with it. She was laughing at him mockingly. The fighting continued. Tony broke the glass in the kitchen door window when he pushed her head through it.

I left the house, wanting no part of this action. I was not sure what Tony would do to me once he found out that it was me who had told his wife what he had been up to.

Tom drove me past the house several hours later. All seemed calm. I knew I would have to face them sooner or later, and it might as well be now. I thanked Tom for the ride and went inside.

Tony, without commenting on my leaving or returning, instructed me to help Becky pack. "The BITCH is moving out tonight."

After packing her bags and loading the car, Tony stood in the doorway with his middle finger in the air, waving and yelling out, "Good riddance!" He turned around and looked at me. "You can get a job, or get out too!"

Chapter Eight—The Pervert

I TRIED LOOKING FOR WORK and lying about my age. I said I was sixteen when I was really only fifteen. After searching for days for a retail position at the La Mirada Mall and being rejected again, I walked home. A few blocks away from the house, Tom drove up and offered me a ride the rest of the way. Tony was furious when he looked out the kitchen window and saw me getting out of the car. He wasted no time, running to embarrass me and accusing me of "sleeping around" all day instead of looking for a job.

I was disgusted with him and Becky for always accusing me; I had no intention of having sex. For one, I didn't know what the big deal was. I hated it. Two, I had heard the way guys talked about girls who did give into sex. Also, I believed at that time that guys could tell if you were a virgin. I was terrified someone would find out I wasn't a virgin—thanks to my father.

Angelo sent twenty to forty dollars via money order about every other week to help pay schooling expenses and as hush money to keep me quiet. The money went, instead, to Tony's drugs. But all he ever complained to me about was how expensive it was to have another mouth to feed and take care of. So I cashed the checks, and he took the money. Once in a while, I got a few bucks when Tony played the big shot.

With Becky now out of the way, Tony pranced around with such arrogance and cockiness that he caused a stir wherever he was. He continued to act out his relentless, aggressive, and ruthless ways. His personality changed rapidly, going from weird or funny to mean-spirited, controlling, and paranoid. When ulcers caused him to cut back on his drinking, his drug use escalated. Drinking and playing with the minds of others in a mean and spiteful manner became his favorite pastimes. When he became bored or had no one else to talk to, he would wake me from my sleep at all hours of the night. Sitting on the bed and staring at me, he caused the hair to rise on the back of my neck. His favorite game of torture was to whisper softly in my ear, "Sandra, are you sleeping?" He whispered my name over and over again, "Sannnnnn-dra, Sannnnnndra." Disguising his voice, he made different sounds—sometimes in a childlike way, other times in a deep, eerie way.

I tried to ignore him, hoping he would just go away. I pleaded with him to leave me alone. But he wouldn't stop until I agreed to get up with him. So, giving in to his badgering, I would get up and sit with him and do drugs while he went into one of his many dictatorial, egotistical speeches, professing "I am—Tony Cicero. Do you know how superior and great I am?"

He would rant and rave like a fire-and-brimstone Baptist preacher. I was now taking speed to stay awake, and downers to sleep. We sat and smoked hash or pot, listening to the radio or TV until he wanted to get some sleep.

Tony was becoming extremely paranoid; he was hearing "hidden messages in the music." Stopping and replaying the music over and over, he would ask me if I "heard the message."

His paranoia led him to put a tape recorder in the air duct system of the house. He set it up to be noise- or voice-activated in an attempt to catch his wife sneaking into the house.

Instead I got caught having parties in the house. Tony had taped one of the parties. One night he woke me from a sound sleep, and once again conned me into getting up and listening to music with him and smoking pot. After the song was over, he got up and put on another tape. I thought I was losing my mind. I could hear voices. I closed my eyes and opened them again, looking around the room. Where were the voices coming from?

Tony, of course, played it out as long as he could. When the tape was finished playing, he just sat there watching me and let the tape run out and shut off. Then, he leaned forward and in his most aggressive voice slowly and loudly began to raise his voice. Only inches from my face, I could smell the alcohol on his breath: "You think you're so damn smart! Who the hell do you think you're dealing with, little sister?"

Stunned and unable to move, I didn't respond.

Tony was on his feet pacing back and forth as he barked out again: "Answer me!"

He hammered on, offering to play the tape again for me. I was putting the pieces together, and realized once again that "my brother" had outsmarted me and had somehow taped one of the parties. "Big deal, so you busted me—who cares!"

Surprised by my answer, he laughed. He wanted me to start having more parties so he could tape them. He wanted to see if he could hear people "getting it on" in the bedroom. And he continued to make fun of all people. "They are all stupid!"

It shouldn't have surprised me that a man who made fun of his wife, beat her up, and put down all women would say: "All you women have to do is spread your legs and you get whatever you want."

I was baffled and afraid of him, and worked very hard at trying to stay on his good side. I didn't want him to think that I was like the women he spoke of. My friends all made jokes about him. I became increasingly annoyed and mimicked his behavior when he wasn't around. But I walked on eggshells when he was, hoping his rage would not turn on me.

Meanwhile, Gracie and Tiffany looked good on the outside. They had the nice home in the suburbs, a mom and a dad, food and clothes. Yet Linda and I questioned why Gracie somehow seemed so unhappy. Then, Gracie ran away from home one more time and her father had her placed in a mental hospital—she was only fourteen.

Once, when Gracie and I were getting loaded together, she had mentioned to me, "I'm married to my dad."

Not trusting my instincts at the time, I dismissed her comment. But now I wondered if Mr. Rogers had been sexually abusing Gracie.

Fear ran through me. If Gracie ended up in a mental hospital, it could happen to me.

Linda and I began spending more time together, and less time with Tom and his friends. Linda was furious with me when I suggested one day that Mr. Rogers—who we both thought was crazy and bizarre—was having an affair with her mother. This turned out to be true. Eventually, he left his wife and married Linda's mother.

Mrs. Rogers ran off and disappeared after the divorce, and Tiffany went to live with a neighbor who felt sorry for her since she was left alone so much.

Life was becoming more and more of a blur for me. I didn't like myself and struggled to feel sane. Nothing made sense. I tried to talk to Linda on occasion, questioning the meaning of life. She usually laughed at me and told me I spent too much time thinking. Using drugs was the only thing that made sense to me. That way, I didn't have to feel anything that was going on around me.

Tony and I were getting stoned or high together daily, even though I hated getting loaded with him. It was a fight for me to keep up with his every word or movement. I didn't trust him for one second, but knew if I wanted to keep peace in the house I had to do as I was told and to pretend that I enjoyed his company.

It was my job to continue to keep the house cleaned, wash the clothes, and cook all the meals. But Tony only demanded more and more from me, including that I quit school and get a job to help support myself and the payments on his house.

As much as I dreaded being in his home, I was relieved that he did not want to send me back to Cleveland. His mood swings were happening more frequently. One minute he would try to be funny or friendly. And the next, he might jump up and yell, "Get the hell out of my house!"

His unpredictable mood swings increased. He was changing jobs, getting fired, and telling me how lucky I was to be a woman. Tony continued to bully me with his grandiose, delusional ideas about himself. I was embarrassed to be seen with him. He was a devious and manipulative liar.

He sang along with Paul McCartney or Rod Stewart into his imaginary microphone. And he would grab his crotch and rub it, making up his own words to the songs: "All you women want is this." Night after night, he held me hostage with his circus. I grew exhausted after more than a year of his constant bantering and torture. I knew "it" was going to happen, with or without my approval. It was only a matter of time.

One night, Tony convinced me to try some different pills. When I questioned him as to what they were, he snapped at me, "When did you get so picky about free drugs?"

Switching to his "mister nice guy" personality, he followed his last comment with, "Oh come on, Sannnnn-dra, try it. I heard these are a really great high."

The last thing I remember about that night was a feeling of suffocation as I came in and out of reality—with him on top of me.

My brain is hazy on how I ended up in a La Mirada park that night.

Chapter Nine—Overload

THE ROOM SEEMED HAZY when I opened my eyes. Nothing looked familiar, but it didn't look like my idea of purgatory, heaven, or hell either. Startled by the sight of a woman sitting next to me, I waited for her to speak.

She had been praying for me for several hours as I recovered from an apparent drug overdose. Realizing that we were not alone in the room, I tried to sit up. But I found my head was still spinning, and I was forced to lie back down. Jacque introduced herself and two others in the room, her daughters Lynn and Kim. She then went on to say, "I guess you already know my son, Greg."

I wasn't sure of anything at that moment. Who was Greg? I didn't say anything.

Jacque proceeded to tell me that I was welcome to stay in her home as long as I needed to, but that she would not permit drug use. She also made it very clear that I would go to school every day, but she did not press me at that time for information about why Greg had found me passed out and lying in a park. Ashamed and embarrassed, I couldn't even begin to try to explain to her. And besides, I only vaguely remembered why—but not how.

I told her briefly that my family lived in Cleveland, and that I lived with my brother who had had a drug problem for almost a year. Not knowing what she would do, I pleaded with her not to call the police on me or my brother. She assured me that everything would be all right—that I would be safe in her home.

I fought back the tears—humiliated as I remembered what Tony had done to me. I closed my eyes and blamed myself for agreeing to take the pills. Maybe if I wasn't loaded, I could have fought him off. Pushing away my anger, I thanked Jacque for offering a place for me to stay and hide.

Greg had found me semi-conscious, loaded on drugs in the park, when he tripped over a body in the grassy area on his way home. After looking closely at the body, he recognized me from school. Picking me up and carrying me to his house, he placed me in the garage. It had been converted into a game room for Greg and his friends, and his parents rarely entered.

Jacque explained to me that she had no reason to go out there that night, yet she couldn't shake off the strong feeling to go. She was surprised to find a girl sleeping—passed out—on the couch next to the pool table.

Jacque was a spiritual person and involved in the Jesus Movement of the sixties and early seventies. She had large gatherings of local kids in her home each week for Bible studies. She had a generous heart, and helped out many of the confused kids in the neighborhood by opening her heart and home to all in need.

Greg, I later found out, was very popular with the girls in school. They all loved his charm and casualness as he walked around the school in his white loafers and Levi's, singing as he strummed on his imaginary guitar. We had great fun together—even though, at times, we fought like a brother and sister. We attended Jacque's Bible studies at her request to please her, but then would climb out the window afterward to get high.

Greg's sister, Lynn, converted to Christianity and worked diligently to "save my soul."

She convinced me to go with her to Calvary Chapel in Costa Mesa. I usually got loaded before I went. One night during services at the church, they were discussing Jeremiah in the Old Testament. A tune came into my head, "Jeremiah was a bullfrog. . . "

I thought I was only humming it, but Lynn nudged me to be quiet. I was singing it out loud.

I tried Jacque's patience on numerous occasions—jumping in the La Mirada water fountain, thinking it was a lake, and being taken home by the police one morning for walking down La Mirada Boulevard with a friend in our pink bathrobes we had received as Christmas presents from Jacque.

Lynn was always great to me, offering clothes and helping me with my hair. Lynn was definitely ahead of her time. She was wild and passionate about everything she said or did. She was a beautician and tried out many new ideas, coming up with the wildest styles in hair and fashion. Lynn worked long hours three days a week, and took four days off for the weekend. Even when she wasn't working, she cut the hair of anyone who would let her. Most of La Mirada had their hair cut by Lynn in a shag hairstyle.

She was very kind and took me along for the ride on many of her trips. We went to the mountains or Palm Springs. Lynn had a way of making friends wherever she went. When not cutting hair, she loved singing and playing Christian music on her guitar.

Jacque loved the color orange. Now, I had heard people say, "Oh, what's your favorite color?" from time to time. But she gave new meaning to having a favorite color. Everything in the house was decorated in bright orange—the vinyl backing on the kitchen chairs, the living room sofa, her bedspread, towels, glass ashtrays, you name it. And at Christmas time the tree was not only decorated in huge orange bows and ornaments, but it hung upside down from the ceiling.

I finally decided to try Christianity. The deciding factor came one evening in the kitchen after a Bible study. I had been living with the McClure family for over a year. I answered the telephone and did not respond when I heard his voice. Instead, I handed the phone over to Jacque without speaking.

Tony decided to put his house on the market and, of all the Realtors listed in the phone book, he called McClure Realty. I had managed to hide from him, even though he showed up regularly at school and at some of my friends' houses looking for me. He would threaten my friends, telling them that if they knew where I was or if they were hiding me, when he found me he would not only break my legs but their legs as well.

That night Jacque convinced me to move to a Christian house in Oregon. I was willing to do whatever it took to get away from Tony. I left California on a bus the next day for a twelve-hour ride to Eugene.

Chapter Ten—Shiloh

THE BUS CAME TO A STOP inside the Eugene Greyhound station in the early afternoon. I felt both panic and excitement from being somewhere different—somewhere unknown to me, and somewhere unknown to Tony. I had to get out of California—sure that he was searching for me, wanting to silence me about the rape. Jacque had instructed me how to get to the Shiloh house and gave me a one-way ticket to get there. I had a plan of my own, or so I thought. Once in Oregon, I had planned to explore Eugene before checking myself into wherever it was that I had agreed to go. Putting my one suitcase in a rented locker at the station, I headed out on my new adventure—traveling on foot with ten dollars in my pocket.

I walked two blocks before coming to a guy who was sitting on the porch of a two- story Victorian home, playing a guitar. Stopping to listen as he sang, I smiled and he smiled back. He played and finished the song, then rested the guitar on his lap. After the exchange of a few words, I mentioned that, yes, I was new in town; and that, no, I didn't need a place to stay. I was going to be staying with some friends. I hoped that he wouldn't ask any more questions, for fear he would discover I didn't have a clue about what I was doing or about these friends I had mentioned. I did decide to ask him if he knew of a place called Shiloh. His smile broadened. "Well, Sandy, praise the Lord. You have just arrived at Shiloh."

I tried not to show my shock and disappointment. I guess being on my own for a while was not meant to be. Following him inside the house, I was introduced to Pastor John. He was expecting me, since Jacque had called ahead to inform him of my pending arrival. The pastor introduced me to the deaconess, Dru, and explained she was overseeing the women's house that was located around the corner from 1010 High Street.

Dru had medium dark hair and looked tougher and older than her twenty years. Like many of the others living in Shiloh, Dru was also a runaway and had been living in the commune for a few years. She was dressed in a long, handmade tapestry dress. All the Sisters in Christ wore long, ankle-length dresses. Makeup and short skirts were frowned upon. This would cause our Brothers in Christ to lust after us. Even the thought of lusting after another person was a sin.

I followed her without questioning anything as we walked to my new home; I wished she would slow down her pace. Eugene was beautiful in June. The streets were lined with large oak trees. I was enjoying the surroundings as I took in the sights. I thought about my original plan and was disappointed I didn't have the chance to follow through with it. I was only half listening to what Dru was saying, something about God.

The women's house was quite different from the house we had just left. This house was a single-story ranch home and cut from the same cookie cutter as the other houses in the tract. The only exceptions were the various colors of pastel paint and trim. Once inside the front door, I stood still for a moment, looking at what was to become my new home. I had seen a lot of different living conditions in my time, but this was the oddest setup I had come across. The rooms were covered, not in wall-to-wall carpet, but rather wall-to-wall, handmade wooden bunk beds that were stacked three high starting in the living room. The two bedrooms were also lined with triple bunk beds. Worldly possessions were not acceptable.

"Hoarding material things" was another sin, with good reason— no storage. Each person could only keep what fit into her own personal wooden orange crate. The opening was covered in a tapestry material stapled to the crate, and also stacked three-high on the floor next to the sets of beds. The house had only one bathroom to be shared by fifteen to twenty-five sisters. I was relieved to get assigned a bed closest to the floor and the bathroom.

The other followers were certainly a happy flock, singing, praying, and speaking in tongues. (I never did master that one.) All chores were done with a spirit that reminded me of the seven little dwarfs, singing "Hi-ho, hi-ho, it's off to preach we go."

I did manage to stay amused most of the time, saving my jokes for the new converts who had not yet lost their sense of humor.

The men's house served as the main house where all the meals were prepared, and as the place for witnessing every transient, local druggie, or hippie who came through town and was looking for a free meal. After the "free meal," we had Bible studies to convert new members into the commune—asking not only for them to turn their will and their lives over to God, but all of their personal belongings as well.

Obtaining enough food to feed the multitudes was not as easy as the fish story. Lacking knowledge of how Jesus did this, we started our mornings out in the big, brown Helms truck, stuffing in as many of the followers that could fit for the morning food run. The "food run" involved me and a couple of others being hoisted into a Dumpster located behind the local grocery store, rummaging for food items before the trucks came to empty the trash bins. We found crates filled with day-old fruit and vegetables that had been tossed out merely because they had a minor blemish or two. It's amazing how many different kinds of soup we created. However, after two weeks on a steady diet of cucumber soup, I don't think I was as impressed. And after a year of peanut butter sandwiches with crystallized honey for lunch every day, this too got difficult to swallow. The others kept up their humming spirit. But I questioned if this was really where God had intended me to live out my life.

Each day was the same. After the morning food run, breakfast was served. This was followed by a morning prayer and Bible study. Next, the sisters gathered to clean and prepare all the meals for both houses. The brothers went out to work for the local area growers. Some planted trees, and others picked fruit or vegetables depending on what was in season. Another group went "chicken picking."

The chicken ranches force-fed the chickens, turning the lights off and on, tricking the birds to eat again. The brothers were hired to do the slaughtering. Reaching under the chickens while they were sleeping, they quickly grabbed their feet and turned them upside down. The blood rushed to the chickens' heads, causing them to pass out just before their heads were sliced off. I hated being in the kitchen when the brothers returned home. Their shirts, arms, and faces were covered with bloodstains.

All the daily earnings were pooled together, and the money was turned over to the pastor of the house. It was amazing to see what could be accomplished by promoting the idea to your flock that material wealth is not God's purpose for us here on planet Earth. The powers-that-be at Shiloh were able, in a short time, to purchase one hundred acres of pine tree–covered property in Dexter, Oregon. The property became known as The Land and it was used for Shiloh's main headquarters. Tiny, hand-built cabins housed four to six people in each. A main lodge, big enough for seventy-five or a hundred people, was located in the center. The lodge was equipped with a restaurant-sized kitchen and a main dining area with rows of wood picnic tables and benches. This is where everyone gathered for Bible studies, training, and meals.

Teams of followers, made up of four or five brothers and one sister, were sent here for training. After their training, the teams would hitchhike to different cities around the country where they would set up new Shiloh "houses" and preach their version of the Bible. At one time, Shiloh operated thirty-six of these communal living houses in twenty cities from California to Oregon and as far east as St. Louis.

I pleaded with the pastor to let me work out in the fields after months of being in the kitchen. Only two other sisters wanted to go with me. The others felt that this was man's work. I didn't care; I'd be outside. Working in the fields came to an end for me when I entered high school in September of 1971 as an eleventh grader. I was the only Shiloh member who was young enough to be attending school.

As a school project, I brought in a film someone had made that showed the Shiloh houses and The Land. I was excused from my regular classes for a week and went around to different classes, showing the film and answering questions about what it was like living in a commune. I enjoyed the attention I got from the other kids and the opportunity to get out of my regular classes.

On more than one occasion, some of the other followers tried to persuade me to drop out of school. They informed me that the information taught in public schools would lead only to serving the ways of the flesh, and not help me in serving the Lord. In spite of the pressure, I continued to go. School kept me in touch with reality—that Shiloh's "way" was not the only way to live.

But not having anywhere else to live, I kept my opinions and doubts about Shiloh to myself. To avoid returning to the house right away, I would often take the scenic route home from school. I enjoyed being outdoors and finding a place to hide and be alone. I had discovered a wooded area and went there as much as I could. Sitting by a stream, daydreaming, enjoying the fragrance of the woods, and watching the water flow over the rocks, I was able during these moments to believe that maybe God did exist. But the confusion and tears would inevitably come, and I would question this God about what was to become of me.

Part of our mission in Shiloh was to go door to door or hang out in local shopping centers, preaching the word of God according to Shiloh. We also delivered food items to our neighbors, hoping to preach to them. Promotion, not attraction, brought in countless new members.

One day, we went to a house around the block and tried to witness to a guy in his early twenties. Making fun of us as we gathered at his door and handed him a loaf of bread, he called back into the house, "Hey you guys, I thought you were going to order a pizza. There are some chicks out here with a loaf of bread and no sauce."

My eyes were fixed on the beer bottle in his hand. I hadn't seen a beer, joint, newspaper, or listened to music other than the three chords played on a guitar when we sang "Yes, Jesus loves me," for over a year. Dru, the deaconess, hurried us away from the house.

The next day, I was in the backyard, hanging the laundry to dry. The same neighbor, whose backyard faced ours, sat watching me for a while before yelling out, "Hey sister, you got any more of that bread?"

My heart leaped at the opportunity to do a "good deed," or at least the chance to get out of doing the chores. I just knew that God was calling me there to save his soul. Hurrying into the house, I located my Bible, some bread, and headed over to witness to my neighbor.

Once inside of his house, he requested to see my Bible. Opening it, he proceeded to show me that Jesus turned water into wine. "Why would he do that if he did not want us to drink wine?" he questioned me.

I had only one response, "You're right! And yes, I will share a glass of wine with you!"

He extended the glass toward me and I took it without a thought of what my sisters might think. My newfound friend continued to explain to me more interesting facts about the Bible that Shiloh had failed to mention—like how God had created the heavens, the Earth, the stars, and everything on the planet. "Did he not also create pot, a living natural plant?" he said.

Made sense to me. And with that, my now better-acquainted friend and I smoked a joint.

Putting the Bible aside, he cranked up the stereo and we continued to get inebriated.

I was feeling no pain.

We sipped the day away, and it was nightfall before I began walking—mostly stumbling—back through the yard to get to Shiloh.

Opening the front door, I walked in on fifteen or so sisters who were praying for the devil to be removed from my body.

This was more than I could handle.

And the nice, shy, obedient follower that they were accustomed to was gone. Now stood Sandy, a very defiant drunk.

I told them what they could do with their God and their Bible.

Fortunately for me, I had made friends with a classmate at school. Debbie's family allowed me to move in with them after Debbie explained the sad state of my life to her folks. They agreed a girl my age should not be left on her own. After staying with them for a short while, Debbie and I went to see the newly released film The Godfather. The movie made me think of my family, and the next day, without stopping to question my own sanity, I packed up my guitar and black leather coat, borrowed forty dollars, and hitchhiked back to Cleveland one week shy of completing the eleventh grade.

I had not been in Cleveland in over four years and had lost track of the family. After looking up "Cicero" in the phone book, I found a listing for a relative, Uncle Guido. They were surprised to hear from me and invited me over to the house. Not even thinking of Amy as an option, I was relieved to be staying with Uncle Guido and Aunt Edith again.

Alfredo was the only one of their children still living at home. His brothers and sister had married. The insanity in the house had not changed. Guido was still getting in someone else's face about something. Edith was still waiting on him hand and foot.

I stayed with them a few weeks before finding a furnished apartment of my own.

It didn't take long before I heard about and got involved with my father and the boys. Time was moving on and life was repeating itself. I did not want what they had.

Chapter Eleven—Master Manipulators

I COULD ONLY SHAKE MY HEAD when I heard the news that Angelo had started an electrical company and was now in business, working with a partner—Tony.

Tony, playing the big shot, had remarried his ex-wife, Becky. Together, they had returned to Cleveland after winning a lawsuit against Becky's company. She had fallen at work, causing her to go into premature labor and giving birth to a daughter. Tony, of course, pounced right on the opportunity to make some money, and hired an attorney to sue the company. He collected over twenty thousand dollars, and with the money returned to Ohio to impress the family. The money went fast. Part of it was used to drive back to Cleveland in a white Corvette, purchase electrical supplies, and to open Cicero & Sons Electrical Services. They all shared an apartment together— Tony, Becky, the baby, and Angelo.

Tony enjoyed all the benefits of owning his own company. He thought he didn't have to do any of the work himself. Tony made a grave mistake in underestimating his father. Angelo was not about to play patsy to anyone, especially his son. After about six months, Angelo told him to take a hike. Like the "pot calling the kettle black," Angelo complained that Tony was "the laziest bastard he had ever met."

Angelo, not needing an excuse, seized the opportunity to go out on a drinking binge.

Tony was running out of money fast. Payments were due on the furniture he had purchased and his other expenses were piling up. He did what came naturally to him. He sold off the unpaid-for furniture and left the state, returning to California.

Angelo's patterns hadn't changed since he had gotten out of prison. He charmed everyone in town into giving him credit and had bar tabs in almost every bar in the neighborhood. When he couldn't squeeze another dime out of anyone, he went to work just long enough to pay the bar bills, put some money back in his pocket, and sit back down to drink.

He met Lois after answering a call on an electrical job. He used the same con he had used for years, only this time it paid off: "Hello, is your mommy home?"

Lois, widowed, had saved every penny available from her first husband. She had been living alone for a few years when the electricity in the house began causing many problems. The wiring was old and needed to be replaced. She was delighted when the electrician showed up at her house. She was about ten years older than Angelo and flattered that this handsome, black-haired man was flirting with her. Angelo was eager to get to know this woman a lot better. Even though she was not much to look at, she doted on his every word. Lois invited him in each day for sandwiches for lunch and a home-made meal for dinner. But the real attraction for Angelo was that she paid cash for the work he had done—six thousand dollars. They were married shortly afterward.

Lois discovered soon after the "I do's" that she had not married a gold mine, but a full-blown alcoholic. She tried everything to get him to work. His behavior was the same as always, but new to his third bride.

She called me several times, crying hysterically, "Your daddy is trying to kill me!"

I felt sorry for her, and at times went over to the house to help her out. Once, I had to take a gun away from Angelo after he shot a hole through the bedroom wall—supposedly aiming for Lois on the other side.

Lois then tried giving him the cure. She purchased a case of whiskey and kept a bottle at his bedside. Angelo lay in bed and drank around the clock, not even getting out of bed to pee. Lois just handed him a bedpan. Less than two weeks went by before he became so sick the paramedics had to be called in. Angelo was admitted to a hospital detox program. He stayed for sixty days. Lois was willing to spend the money to save her second husband, hoping to get the money back once he was up and able to return to work.

Lois did her best to keep the business going. She answered the telephones and set up appointments for him.

Angelo never returned to alcohol, but he also never gave up his self-medication on the "Valium maintenance program." He had doctors from the neighborhood, doctors from the VA hospital, and Lois's doctors writing prescriptions for all the drugs he could get. Angelo had so many pills that he started selling them to the neighborhood kids, his nephews, and giving me whatever I wanted. His "good behavior" was wearing thin. He was back to his old tricks—lying to Lois, not showing up for jobs, and hanging out in the bars. But now, loaded on pills, he sat and drank coffee.

Angelo somehow manipulated the Veterans Administration office into classifying him as permanently and totally disabled. He now received a check and a care-package of pills each month, and worked only "under the table" when a job came his way.

Lois managed to make the marriage work for almost ten years, but paid a high price. Angelo had wasted away all of her life savings. He conned her, charmed her, and begged her not to leave him, always with the same promise of any addict: "I'll change." She cashed out her life insurance policies to pay the bills, keeping only a twenty-five hundred dollar policy to bury her.

All the money was gone, and the house was all she had left.

Following heart surgery in which she received a pacemaker, Lois returned home. Angelo had promised to take care of her. His idea of taking care of her was to help her self-medicate on his pills.

Within a few weeks, Lois began experiencing heart pains and rushed back to the hospital by ambulance. By the time Angelo and I arrived at the hospital it was too late. Lois had died. I yelled at the doctor in the hallway, "This is your fault. You and the other doctors keep giving my father all these pills."

Lois had always been a kind and generous person. Out of respect and sympathy for her, and knowing my father was incapable of doing anything, I agreed to make the funeral arrangements.

Later that day, Angelo was so loaded on pills that he was unable to hold his head up. He sat slumped forward in the front seat as we drove to the funeral home.

This was my first experience with making funeral arrangements. Sitting in front of the funeral director, I held Angelo's head up by grabbing the back of his shirt collar. The funeral director used every car room sales tactic possible, "We have solid pine or laminated wood. Would you like solid brass handles?"

He went on to add one more "Would you like the . . . ?" I became so livid with him and Angelo that I yelled out, "I don't care about the box; she's not driving this down the street! We have twenty-five hundred dollars to spend and not a dime more. Take it or leave it!"

They took it.

At the services the next day I was surprised to see that so many of Angelo's family members actually bothered to show up. I hadn't seen them since Grandma's funeral in 1979. And to my knowledge, the family had never even met Lois.

Albert was frantic. "Hey Sis, what am I supposed to do?"

"What do you mean, Albert?" I questioned back.

"You know. It's dad's wife's funeral and I am the oldest son."

I nodded my head in agreement with him. "Oh yeah, Albert you're right. You do need to be taking care of things being Italian, and the oldest son! Well, first you need to stand at the front door of the funeral home and greet all the guests as they come in. Now, this is also very important. When they arrive, Albert, you are to take their shoulders in your hands and pull them toward you, gently kissing them once on the right cheek and once on the left cheek. This is the kiss of honor. Remember the order, Albert, so that you don't do the left cheek first. That would be a dishonor and the kiss of death."

I managed to keep a straight face as I made up the role Albert was to play. I really didn't think even Albert was capable of believing all this.

He did.

I watched, in tears from the back of the room—sadly not tears from the loss of Angelo's third wife, but from the sight of Albert positioned at the door, trying to grab onto people and actually kissing them. Most people were so shocked they allowed his behavior, while others quickly pushed him away, glancing back and shaking their heads in disbelief. Guido, however, came in and shoved Albert aside. He confronted Angelo. "What the hell's the matter with your son? Is he queer? What the hell's he doing?"

One look at me told Angelo who put Albert up to this.

I sat in the front row, watching folks sign the guest book and enter the funeral parlor. They approached the casket and knelt down, bowing their heads in silence. Aunt Evie, who was married to one of Father's brothers, sat on my left. I hadn't seen her in fifteen years. In an effort to make small talk, I looked at her and quietly said, "Hi. So how are you Aunt Evie?"

"I wish it were your uncle in that box instead of Lois!" she blurted out, seemingly not caring who might hear.

I turned to my right. Albert's wife sat stiffly with one of their daughters. Before I could say a word, the small child got up from her chair—and in an instant, the mother reached forward, grabbed hold of her daughter, and slammed the child back into the chair. Crying out the child responded, "I only wanted to go and say a prayer for Grandma."

"You pray for the living, not the dead," snapped her mother.

I got up and walked away.

After the services, everyone lined up outside to follow the casket to the cemetery. I forgot my gloves inside and returned to my seat to get them. I was shocked to find two guys trying to force the casket, which was now on the floor, closed. Lois was a large-framed woman and they were having difficulty closing it.

With his leg stretched up and on top of the casket, one man put all his weight into it as though trying to close an overstuffed suitcase.

Once back at the house, Angelo stretched out from one end of the couch to the other, the back of his hand positioned over his forehead while he began in a slow, yet purposeful raspy voice whining about what was to become of him now that Lois was gone. Who would take care of him? He continued on, criticizing the boys, naming them one by one. My skin was crawling by the time he came to my name. With that, I blew up and blasted him. Albert was in the kitchen when he heard my voice growing louder. Pushing back his chair, he raced to the door. I gave him a quick look. "Stay out of this. This is between me and him!" I said, pointing my finger at Angelo, whose eyes widened with the angry tone of my voice.

Confronting him for the first time in my life, I was able to release my rage and anger.

Screaming at him, I asked him what right he thought he had to expect anything from his children after the life he had given us.
And I told him he could rot in hell. He got up from the couch, and this time I was not the frightened twelve-year-old girl he had taken advantage of. I glared at him, and he stepped back FROM ME in fear. Finally looking away from me, he said, "What do you want me to do—say I'm sorry?"

Chapter Twelve—Life in the Fast Lane

THE JULY FOURTH WEEKEND was approaching and Alfredo had invited me to go camping with him and his friends at Lake Chautauqua in New York, where the main attraction was the legal drinking age, eighteen.

Alfredo was intrigued with me—wanting to hear all about me, my travels, and my life in California and Oregon. I was envious of him because he had lived in the same house his whole life. His parents, despising each other or not, were still married. He seemed to know where he was going with his life and had a plan; he was going to college. We both had all the hormones of eighteen-year-olds running wild inside us. The childlike crush we had for each other, coupled with the drugs and alcohol in our systems, led from one thing to another. We spent the holiday weekend drinking and partying around the clock.

No one suspected that Alfredo and I were sneaking around and sleeping together, until one morning after a party a few doors away from Alfredo's house.

His mother had seen his car parked in the friend's driveway all night. Uncle Guido and Aunt Edith were livid when we pulled in their driveway the next morning.

Aunt Edith stood on the porch, screaming and shaking her fist at us. "What the hell are you doing, staying out all night with your cousin? What are the neighbors supposed to think?"

If the neighbors didn't know before, I was sure they knew it then. I stayed in the car while Alfredo went inside. I could hear the screaming but I couldn't make out the words. The next thing I knew, Alfredo came running down the stairs with a suitcase in his hand. We left that morning for Canada.

Alfredo had a friend with a boat who was vacationing there. The three of us stayed in a tent pitched on an island on the French River and got drunk daily. The island's teenagers were very friendly and invited us to join in on their "purple drinking parties," which consisted of emptying whatever booze item you brought into one communal drinking barrel.

We stayed in Canada just over a week. With money running out, we returned to Cleveland. Alfredo moved into my apartment and we lived together only a short while—a month, maybe two—before leaving for South Carolina. Alfredo had heard it was okay to marry your first cousin in South Carolina. I didn't say it out loud but I figured: Why not? We had been keeping it in the family so far, and I wouldn't need to explain my crazy family to my husband—he was part of the insanity.

I had no intention of bringing any children into the Cicero bloodline. And, I did not trust any man enough to give birth for him. Some of the Shiloh doctrine was still ingrained in me, and they preached it was a sin to have sex without being married. My head decided that if we got married, God would overlook the minor discrepancy.

Within two days we were in Myrtle Beach and standing before the justice of the peace. I got a case of pre-wedding jitters and had a hard time controlling my tears of laughter as the preacher spoke. The guy spoke with a heavy Southern accent, and he stuttered, "Do-do you-you Al-Al-Alfredo, ta-take Sa-Sandra toto be yo-your la-lawful wa-wedded wife?"

My spouse-to-be did not see the humor in this, and was annoyed with me before we ever left the services.

Uncle Guido and Aunt Edith were stunned and then furious at the news of our marriage. I became the enemy. How could I do this to their son?

The music played loudly over the car stereo: "If loving you is wrong, then I don't want to be right." I don't think the writers were referring to marrying your first cousin. Oh well, what did I know?

Uncle Guido called our apartment daily, and rudely hung up if I answered the phone. Other times, without so much as a hello, he just barked. I responded to this in kind with, "Alfredo, Uncle Daddy is on the phone."

My new in-laws became "Uncle Dad" and "Aunt Mom."

I worked job after job, sometimes two jobs at a time, trying to pay the rent and put Alfredo through chiropractic school. Coping at the age of eighteen with all the responsibility of a marriage, I grew more and more disgusted with Alfredo—feeling as though I were his mother, not his wife.

Lucky for me, the in-laws decided it was not in their best interest to keep me at a distance—not if they wanted to have Alfredo around. Also, "Uncle Dad" probably figured out that the income I earned would be that much less money he would have to put out to support him.

He became very helpful to me in finding employment. The jobs were tough, but the pay was better than most for a high school drop-out. "Uncle Dad" had contacts with a union. My first job was at a large bakery in Cleveland. I worked on the packaging line, sliding six packages of cupcakes at a time off a conveyor belt and onto large baker trays. I was amazed that some of the long-term workers had this down to a science—one which I had no intention of learning. They had the ability to slide the cupcakes off with one hand and be eating with the other. After putting in ten to twelve hours per day, Alfredo ordered me to quit after four days so I could keep up with my responsibilities at home.

I worked a string of other small-time jobs before I landed another union job. This time I went to work with an automotive parts factory—from cupcakes to brake drums.

The different classes of jobs were based on seniority—pickers, checkers, and packers. I started out as a packer.

All the workers—mostly females—did anything they could to slow the others down while making themselves look better in front of the bosses.

Pickers were paid by the number of orders they filled, not the number of parts per order. So they kissed up to the male bosses to get the fewest amount of items to fill on any one order.

Packers worked in the area known as the "bull pen" and they did take a lot of bull from everyone. The bull pen was located below a steel-floored ceiling. The bosses stood overhead and watched to see that you moved at the pace they expected of you. If you stopped for a moment to scratch an itch, they would stomp their big, black shoes on the steel floor above and yell out, "Get a move on it!"

As if the work wasn't tough enough, workers found various means of torturing each other. Checkers liked to surprise the packers by pushing cartons down the assembly line, causing them to slam into your hands.

I kept this job long enough to do physical damage to my uterus. Lifting brake drums and other heavy auto parts was too much for my 110-pound body to handle. This afforded me time off with pay, and medically provided drugs, which I supplemented with some of my own.

The relationship with the in-laws showed major signs of improvement. "Aunt Mom" volunteered to come over and help to clean the apartment while I was home convalescing. Of course, being afraid of what she might think of me, I forced myself to get up and put the place in order before she arrived.

I tried my hand in the restaurant business for a while, waiting on tables of executives who came in each day for lunch in the private dining room of a greeting card company. This was the first job I did enjoy going to. The head chef and the other woman I worked with were great fun, and I learned some creative cookery skills. I took pride in my work and self for the first time in a long time—cutting apples into birds, and lemons into baskets. We also had to decide which color tablecloth to put on the tables with which napkins. The hours were wonderful—nine until three each day, Monday through Friday. I also got to split any leftovers with the other woman. We ended up each day with steak, chicken, or fish to take home, helping us both with our own food budgets.

But my spouse was not happy driving ten miles to school each day. So, I left the job I enjoyed. We relocated to an Italian community only about half a mile from Case Western Reserve University.

I found work as a receptionist and assistant to the students. Lunch hours were spent at the corner bar, downing vodka martinis with my boss. At night I worked as a waitress, sneaking as many drinks for myself as possible and taking diet pills to work the late shift. I brought home enough money to pay the household expenses, plus put him through school. He worked only during school breaks, picking up odd jobs.

He was demanding and showed signs of becoming a younger version of Guido. The only role models he had were his parents. I kept trying to do things right but felt as though I was living in a commercial most of the time, with him making comments like, "Why aren't these socks as white as my mother gets them?"

As with all the men in my life, he did little to help around the apartment except dictate to me what my role was to be. He was extremely possessive and I couldn't leave the apartment without constant questioning. He not only wanted to know why I was going, but exactly what time I would be returning. Shortly after I would arrive, the telephone would ring and he'd ask, "How long you going to stay there?"

It didn't matter to him if I was sitting in the apartment next door in the same building. He called or came over, asking me to come home. We fought continually. The fights always ended with Alfredo saying, "Sandy, don't leave. It will get better when I'm out of school."

Life was lived by the clock—Alfredo's clock. He informed me each morning what his schedule was for the day, and what time I was to have his meals prepared, or what time I was to drive him to and from school. We now lived four blocks from the school and he insisted I drive his lazy ass to school!

The big highlight of my day was learning what time I was going to be laid that night. He was so considerate, informing me of the time each of the evening's events were to happen. "I will need to study until. . . , eat at. . . , and WE can 'fool around' from nine to nine thirty, maybe even nine forty-five, but then I'll have to get up and study." I really resented this and asked if we could start and finish our "fooling around" earlier. The evening movies always started at nine and I hated to miss the first half-hour. We had a digital clock where the numbers flipped down to indicate the passing minutes. I watched each minute pass, waiting anxiously for the minute that I could tap Alfredo on the shoulder and say, "Time's up."

Alfredo did not want me drinking or getting loaded without him. It was okay to do it as long as he wanted to get high too. So I usually waited for him to return to his studies in the other room. Then I would sneak out on the porch to smoke a joint, and followed it with a vodka chaser once I was back in the living room. I always kept a pint of vodka hidden in the sofa.

Becoming more and more dependent on the booze and diet pills to get me through each day, I told myself that the pills kept me alert for working nights, and that "a few" drinks before I left my shift at two or three in the morning would help me to unwind and get some sleep before returning to my daytime job.

We had gone away once again to Lake Chautauqua for the 4th of July, and I walked into our tent only to find Alfredo naked on top of one of my girlfriends. They were too busy to even notice my presence. Stunned, I walked away, picked up a fifth of Black Velvet, and proceeded to get smashed. I never said a word to either of them. Alfredo and I drove home in silence. I was tired of having to pretend everything was all right.

On the Monday morning following the trip, I sat at the kitchen table writing down my weekly grocery list and wondered what I was doing. Realizing how much I hated my life, I could not bring myself to go through one more day shopping for food, squeezing tomatoes, lying to myself that things would work out for us. Crumbling the grocery list and picking up the phone, I called one of the few friends I had.

"Hi Debbie. This is Sandy. Can you give me a ride to the airport?"

"What?"

"Debbie, please don't ask any questions. Will you drive me or not?"

"Why," she paused, "I guess so."

I had tried to leave once before, driving off in my 1968 Falcon with one working headlight and bad brakes. I made it as far as Kansas and turned around.

"I am leaving Cleveland. Now, please hurry." My heart was beating faster. I could feel the adrenaline pumping through my veins. I raced around the apartment, packing only one small suitcase. I took one last glance at the apartment and hurried for the door. The telephone began ringing. I stopped, looked at the phone, and continued for the door, letting it ring. Debbie pulled up in front of the apartment building just as I walked out. I got in the car.

She started asking me questions. "What are you doing?"

"I told you that I don't want to talk about it. I just can't stand living this way anymore."

"But what about Alfredo?" she asked.

"I can't think about him any more. I can't think about any of this. If I don't get away now, I'll go insane."

Inside, the anger was becoming stronger. Why was everyone so concerned about Alfredo? What about me? The thoughts burned in my mind. "He can just go to hell."

A storm front had been moving in all morning. The weather was getting much worse outside. I stared at the windshield wipers, turning my thoughts to them and keeping my mind off the matter at hand. I hated the hot, humid July storms. I changed the radio station to listen for the news. The wind and rain were making it increasingly difficult for Debbie to keep the car on the road. Suddenly, the car swerved and slammed into the curb. A hole in the road forced us to stop. We were fine but the car couldn't be driven. The front tire had been wedged into the fender.

"Damn!" I screamed.

"Now what?" Debbie asked.

Debbie needed to call for a tow truck. I needed to get to the airport. "Debbie, I'm sorry but I must go now. I can't wait for a tow."

I opened the door and got out of the car, then waved down the first cab. "Good-bye, Debbie. Thanks."

All flights out of Cleveland had been delayed. My fear was that Debbie had gone to a telephone, calling Alfredo to stop me. I trusted no one. Sitting at the bar drinking, I waited for the announcement that the storm had let up and that my flight was now boarding. Once the plane was in the air, I started to breathe a little easier.

I took only enough money out of our savings for airfare, plus one hundred and fifty dollars to live on. I had no idea what was in store for me, returning to California at twenty-two years old; I was not in touch with how much more expensive life in California would be. I had learned to live on twenty-five dollars a week to feed the two of us. Our rent was sixty-five dollars a month, all utilities included. I earned about three hundred dollars a month at the university and a second job as a waitress to make ends meet.

The stewardess came over to me. "Can I get you anything?"

"Yes, you can get me a double scotch rocks."

When she returned with my drink, I reached up and removed the diamond heart necklace I was wearing. I placed it on her tray and said, "This is yours if you can keep me in scotch till this plane lands in Los Angeles."

"Why, no problem." She put the necklace in her pocket.

The no smoking sign came on. "Please put your seat belts on. We will be landing in just a few moments."

I was feeling no pain. Numb from the alcohol, I carefully walked off the plane.

I arrived back in California in July of 1976. With no plans for what to do next, I checked into an airport hotel. After being gone for several years, I was too excited to sit there alone. I had to call someone and my brother was the only person I knew to call. Tony answered the phone. "Where the hell are you?"

When I told him I was in California, his tone changed. "I'll send Becky to pick you up."

And she did.

The first few days, other than smoking a lot of pot and drinking day and night, became a blur for me. Tony and Becky never recovered from losing all their money and the house in La Mirada. Tony went into car sales, selling mostly on used car lots. He had gone downhill fast after his return from Ohio, and they moved from one rental to another. It was up to Becky to either earn enough money, or borrow the money from her family, to keep them going.

He and Becky fought constantly, leaving Becky with bruises or black eyes. She had lost any self-respect she had long ago, as well as any respect she had for Tony, but continued to stay in the marriage. Their child was one year old at the time. I ended up staying with Becky while Tony was in county jail, serving a sixty-day sentence for drunk and disorderly.

I called Alfredo three weeks later. "You'd better go grocery shopping. I'm not coming back."

We divorced. Alfredo took care of all the details. In Cleveland, there was no such thing as a no-fault divorce. So he sued me for desertion and not fulfilling my wifely duties. He kept all of the furniture and other possessions we collected during the marriage. Alfredo was generous enough to ship me my clothes and the only other items he had no use for—a box of pots and pans. After all, he had his mother to cook and clean for him once again.

Chapter Thirteen—Collision Course

THE MUSIC OF HALL & OATES played loudly on the radio. I knew the lyrics by heart: "The weak give up and stay, while the strong give up and move on." Indeed, I had. I moved from Cleveland to Southern California July 11, 1976. I told myself that I was going to do anything and everything I had been told my whole life I couldn't do "because you're a girl," "because you're Italian," or better yet, "because you're Catholic."

I stayed out every night drinking and taking drugs, sleeping or passing out in my car, most nights too drunk to drive or find my way home.

I found a job as a parts driver for an auto dealer in Huntington Beach. This gave me transportation and freedom to run around, to come and go as I pleased. I started each morning on Beach Boulevard, stopping at a McDonald's to purchase a large Coke. Only wanting the cup, I poured out the soda after only a sip or two, then proceeded to the liquor store across the street and purchased a pint of Southern Comfort. Once the plastic cup was filled, I drove into work sipping on breakfast while the truck was being stocked for the day's route. Each day, I made the route as quickly as possible. Usually by ten o'clock in the morning my cup ran empty, so I stopped in Hof's Hut and switched to scotch—no ice. After a few drinks I went into the bar-area bathroom and changed out of my blue work shirt and Levi's into a dress and high heels—going out for interviews, hoping to locate a better job.

I closed the bars each night and woke abruptly most mornings to the ringing of the telephone. I was getting livid with my soon-to-be ex-husband for constantly calling me once he discovered I was staying at my brother's—trying to convince me to return to him and promising that he would change. What he really wanted was his meal ticket back.

The calls usually came around 6 a.m. and I had to run out to the living room and grab the phone, stopping the ringing before it woke Becky and the baby. "Leave me alone. Don't you get it? I'm not coming back to you or Cleveland," I barked into the receiver.

"Hello, is this the Cicero residence?" the caller questioned.

"Yes, who is this?" I replied.

"I'm a friend of Tony's and he gave me this number, telling me to call for a ride home—that either his sister or his wife would help me out."

"Well, this is his sister and I'm not giving anybody a ride anywhere. Hold on, I'll get his wife!"

Throwing the phone down on the couch, I called out for Becky. Becky, being the obedient wife no matter the circumstance, left to pick up some guy from county jail to give him a ride home. My brother just met this guy in jail and gave him his home phone number.

I was glad to have Becky out of the house that morning so I could light up a joint. I started every morning since arriving back in California with a drink and pot. On some mornings, I added a line of coke to take the edge off the hangover from the night before. I was getting by on three or four hours sleep a night—staying in the bars after work until they closed and pushing myself to just get home so I could crawl into bed before passing out. Some nights I came to parked in the driveway, asleep on the front seat. Other nights, I woke to find myself parked on a side street—only a few blocks from home.

I sat down on the living room couch and put my feet up on the coffee table. Putting the bottle of beer next to the ashtray, I began to roll a joint. I looked at the clock. Shit, I was going to be late again. I inhaled deeply for one last hit on the joint. The front door opened and in walked Becky. She was not alone. Following behind her was a guy about thirty years old. His eyes stared at my half-naked body.

Trying to gather my thoughts and hide my surprise at their sudden appearance, I finally responded, "Excuse me, but I wasn't expecting company at seven o'clock in the morning."

Becky rolled her eyes in disapproval and made her own excuses as to why she brought "Brad" home with her from jail. Informing me that he lived close to where I worked, she thought I wouldn't mind dropping him off on my way to work. Furious that she caught me off guard, yet not wanting a scene in front of the now nervous-looking guest, I agreed. Remembering my people-pleasing role in life, I proceeded to offer Brad coffee. Trying hard not to stare at me, he looked away from my see-through nightshirt. He looked down at my beer, asking if he could have one.

Brad was only visiting here in California, and was staying with some friends in Newport Beach. He had been arrested for drunk and disorderly in a bar the night before and thrown in jail to sleep it off.

I worked in Huntington Beach, and Newport was not on the way. But the ride was a blast. We were both pretty stoned by now, having finished off two beers each before leaving the house and smoking a joint on the road. I didn't have a care in the world. This was living. Driving down Pacific Coast Highway with the windows down, music playing loudly on the radio, and the sun shining brightly over the ocean, we drove to the end of a road. I pulled up the long winding driveway as instructed by Brad. I couldn't believe the view. The house was enormous. Just then, the gate opened and we were greeted by Brad's friend, Miles.

He came half running up to the truck. "Brad, you son of a gun. Where the hell have you been? I was expecting you two days ago, alone!" he said, looking at me with a grin.

Brad got out of the truck and I was about to back up when Miles spoke up. "Hey, don't go."

"I have to get going. I'm already late for work and I have to get this truck back in," I replied.

Miles was persistent, explaining to me that he had been on the phone all morning trying to locate a small truck. He was in the process of moving a few things from one store to another in town. I didn't have a clue what he was talking about, but he certainly was excited to be rattling off his problems to me.

I tried, once again, to explain my situation—that the truck was not mine to loan, and I had to get to work. I was also embarrassed to be seen dressed in my blue cotton men's work shirt with the company logo embroidered on the front pocket. Miles finally hit the right button. "Hey, come on in. You interested in doing a line or two?"

I turned off the engine and followed the guys into the house. It was spectacular—a two-story house on the cliffs, overlooking the ocean. I felt as if I were Alice in Wonderland. Just inside the entrance, we walked only about ten feet or so when Miles stopped to open the mirrored closet doors. Pushing them back as they folded back to the sides, he reached out and turned on the lights. I had never seen a bar built inside a closet. The whole thing lit up. Miles pulled open a drawer and withdrew the coke. "Do you mind if I have a drink while you're doing that?" I asked.

"No. Help yourself," he responded.

I poured myself a straight gin. The lines of cocaine were put in front of me, and I snorted them quickly through the dollar bill Brad had rolled up.

Miles asked about the truck again. This time I just laughed and said, "Sure, no problem. Take the truck."

They both thanked me and walked back out the front door, promising to return in less than an hour. Miles showed me where to find the telephone in case I wanted to call in to work. I decided I was having too much fun to ruin the mood by talking to my new boss, who I was sure was very angry by now.

With a drink in one hand and a joint in the other, I slowly walked around from room to room. The house had cathedral ceilings in the kitchen and living rooms, and an indoor fountain with the sound of water pouring over river rocks. Fascinating art pieces and pictures were displayed everywhere. I was in awe, having never seen anything like it—not even in the movies. Not that I was an expert or anything. I was a twenty-two-year-old kid from Cleveland, on the run from a bad marriage, and I had about one hundred dollars to my name. The view from the sliding glass doors was breathtaking.

I sat down on the couch, looking out at the ocean. My thoughts were interrupted by the footsteps coming down the spiral stairs. I watched the legs appear and then the rest of the man's body. He was wearing a white clinical coat, unbuttoned down the front and exposing his naked body underneath. He nodded at me without speaking, and proceeded to the bar to pour a drink. After lighting a cigarette, he walked toward me in the living room. He didn't seem the least bit embarrassed that I was watching him. Twice in one day, I was embarrassed and pretended not to be.

He introduced himself. "Hi. The name's Louis."

"Hi. The name's Cicero."

"No shit! What a great name," he responded.

The next thing I remembered was the front door opening, and Miles and Brad had returned. Standing in the living room, they both started to explain why they had taken so long with the truck. Talking and laughing, each interrupted the other with more details. "We tried to call the house several times today. I can see now why you two didn't bother to answer the telephone."

Louis and I were dancing naked in front of the fireplace, our clothes tossed in a pile on the floor.

That "day" turned into my staying from Thursday till Monday morning. By then, I was getting paranoid that if I didn't return the company truck I could be reported for stealing a vehicle. Louis followed me to Huntington Beach on Monday morning. I told him I'd be all right, but fortunately he didn't listen to me and came along anyway. When I walked through the door of the dealership my boss jumped all over me. "What the hell's the matter with you? Why the hell couldn't you pick up the telephone and call me?"

His voice was getting louder and louder as he screamed at me, looking for answers.

"I don't have to take this attitude from you or anyone," I screamed back. I threw the keys at him and walked out. Louis was all too happy to drive me back to Newport where I stayed for the next two months.

I called Becky and told her not to be expecting me. She tried to lay a guilt trip on me for not calling her sooner. I reminded her that she was not responsible for me, nor was she my mother. Trying to hide my annoyance and resentment with Becky was sometimes difficult. I was still angry with her for the part she played in what took place in La Mirada eight years earlier.

During my stay in Newport, I stayed loaded morning, noon, and night. I drank and took drugs on a daily basis, hanging out at the beach to sleep off the hangovers during the day. Brad returned to Boston after his one-week stay. Miles, Louis, and I went out to dinner nightly and danced until closing in the local bars. We stayed up till three or four o'clock in the morning snorting cocaine. The guys invited people over to the house to party with us. I tried not to question what I was doing or why. Nothing was real. Life was just a game to be played. The guys seemed to have moments of consciousness. I wanted no part of it. I was not going to settle down and think about life or what tomorrow might bring. I was living in a great house, overlooking the ocean. I didn't have to work to support them. We went out shopping, dining, and drinking. They bought me clothes and gifts. This was all very exciting—hanging around with the guys.

Miles announced one day that he and Louis were taking a vacation they had planned before I arrived. The house was listed on the market and Miles wanted to know if I would mind staying in the house to keep an eye on things while they were gone.

Would I mind? I'd be delighted to have this place to myself for two weeks. But, of course, I didn't want him to know that. Instead, I shrugged my shoulders and replied, "Yeah, sure. No problem. It's the least I can do after all you have done for me."

While they shopped at Fashion Island for items for their trip, I sat drinking in a restaurant bar in the mall. During the two hours I waited for them, I met William. He was a tall, quiet, good-looking man dressed handsomely in a suit. And he was confused about the two guys who kept coming in and out of the bar, paying for my drinks. I assured him they were "just friends," and we exchanged phone numbers before I left with the guys.

The next day I drove Miles and Louis to the airport. After returning to the house, I called William. He came over and stayed with me for the next two weeks. During that time he asked me to move out of Newport and move in with him. When the guys returned from their trip, I did.

I found employment in a dental lab and went out drinking nightly with my new "roommate." However, I continued to stay in touch with the guys from Newport. We all went out on New Year's Eve. That's where I met Victor. He was another friend of Louis's from Boston. When my date ended up passed out, face down on the table, I switched over to Victor. We spent the night together, and within a few days I moved to Brentwood and went to work for him in his telemarketing company.

Tony had been out of jail for a few months now and was complaining to me that we never got together. I still couldn't face my anger toward him. Being away from him for a few years had not wiped the memories from my mind. I just drank away the feelings. Not wanting to burn the only family connection I had in California, I finally agreed to take him out. He wanted to see Brentwood and where I was living. I wanted to rub his face in how well I was doing with my life.

I was embarrassed to be seen with him, and we stopped at a bar in town before I took him to meet Victor.

We stayed only briefly. I made some excuse to take Tony home early. Tony was disgusting, and his physical and emotional condition was deteriorating daily as the result of his excessive drinking and drugs over the years. He no longer could command the attention that he did less than eight years ago. People no longer feared his presence. He weighed less than 120 pounds. His face had sunken in, his eyes were bloodshot, and he was still wearing his polyester, bell-bottom pants with imitation silk print shirts. He hadn't held a steady job in years. Becky continued to work and kept his existence going. They could only afford to live in rentals and moved around often.

Tony provoked fights in bars, restaurants, and grocery stores. When others walked past him I cringed, hoping they wouldn't look at us. I knew that he would snap, "What the hell are you looking at?"

When people looked at the skeleton of this man, I saw only pity in their eyes. He was looking more and more as if he were a poster child for "help feed the poor."

We had just driven back into Orange County when a police officer stopped me and gave me a warning ticket because of the exhaust smoke that was coming out of the car. Sighing in relief that this was the only reason he pulled me over, I was polite and thanked him for the warning about the car. I had bought Tony's black Toronado after he was released from jail.

Not wanting to be pulled over again, Tony instructed me to pull into a car lot on Harbor Boulevard. We walked up and down a few aisles with the salesman before picking a silver long sleek Buick to test drive. The salesman was walking around the car to get in with us when Tony yelled out, "Come on, Sandy. Let's get out of here!"

Without questioning him, I followed his instructions and we drove off, leaving the salesman standing on the sidewalk. Working in the business, Tony knew they could not report the car as stolen for twenty-four hours since they had handed me the keys. We spent the next several hours in a bar, and then we returned the car. We were both drunk, and the salesman didn't find us at all amusing even after we agreed to buy the car.

Victor was not pleased when I did not return on the day I left to drive my brother home; instead I returned a few days later. I had no explanation about where I was or why I was now driving a different car. We had been living and working together for over a year. At work I was answering the phones, taking most of the sales calls, and helping out with scheduling for the "boiler room." And at home I did all the chores considered "woman's work."

Victor's drinking and disappearing acts were happening all too frequently. Yet he had the nerve to press me for answers about my actions and whereabouts. I wasn't about to sit back and let him dictate to me, or take advantage of me again. And, without another word, I packed my belongings and moved out that day.

As I left him and drove away, I remembered my vow to myself— that I would do everything and anything I wanted to. No one was going to dictate to me how to live. Even when a voice from within told me I might be completely out of control, I kept moving, sedating myself enough to mask the fear inside. I was making up the rules as I went along. Drinking diminished my feelings of insecurity and anger. I laughed at myself and at others. When the pain became too great, I ran.

Returning to the dealership, I interviewed and was hired for a job at the same place from which I had "borrowed," and later bought, the car. The manager who hired me was not aware that I was the woman who had taken the car from them a few days earlier. I met Taylor, a salesman, the first day on the job. He was medium height and slim with blondish-brown hair. He had that certain smoothness about him, and somehow convinced customers that he was doing them a favor by selling them a car.

Taylor grinned when he recognized me as the woman who had "taken" the car and caused such an uproar. With laughter in his voice, he approached me and invited me out for a drink after work. We began an on-again, off-again relationship, and lived together for the next few years.

I had no idea that the life I was living was so different from others'. I thought everybody in California lived an exciting, wild, carefree existence.

A call came from Ohio to inform me of Grandma Cicero's death. I knew that God was punishing me one more time. Shocked and angry, I did the only thing I knew to do—drink a bottle of brandy and down a few pills. Even with the amount of alcohol in my body, I managed to get back to Cleveland to attend the services. Taylor drove me to the airport and helped me to the plane, making excuses to the attendants for my drunken appearance.

I found myself standing frozen at the back of the funeral home, watching all my aunts and uncles walk up the aisle leading to Grandma's casket. I couldn't face them. I didn't want to see her dead body; I only wanted to run. I wanted to remember her spirit—how she walked me to the store, holding my hand. I wanted to remember the warmth I felt, watching her cook in the kitchen and tell me stories in broken English. I broke out crying.

My brothers couldn't understand my display of emotions. "What's she crying about? People die every day."

I couldn't go to the casket. I felt the eyes watching me. "No respect," whispered my aunt.

The cars lined the street. Seventy-five cars—black limos, Caddies, Oldsmobiles, Buicks—were all in a row, waiting for the procession to begin the long drive through the neighborhood where Grandmother had lived and around the streets to the cemetery.

I, however, was riding with Mario. We were positioned about in the middle, moving through the streets at five miles an hour in his gray-primered, red pickup truck. Here we were in his work truck with all the electrical equipment and conduit pipes hanging out the tail end. Now if things weren't bad enough, we ran out of gas, and stopped the procession. I wanted to crawl under the seat while he and Sam pushed the truck to the side of the road. We climbed into the car that was carrying my father.

Having only been married a short while, Sam's wife, Judy, had not been to any of the Cicero functions. She questioned Sam as to why they were carrying my grandmother everywhere.

"What do you want her to do, walk?" Sam replied.

I returned to California the next day.

I don't think I ever really understood the concept of commission sales. I sort of figured that I was supposed to be at work when my name was on the shift. So what more could they want from me? While most of the salesmen were hustling to sell cars, I was more concerned with finding ways to get off the lot and to the bar around the corner.

In car sales, they also had a policy referred to as "courtesy call." If you had a customer come in to pick up their car while you had the day off, they tried reaching you at home to ask if you wanted to split your commission with the person delivering the car. It was my day off, and I had been relaxing with a joint for breakfast and had also taken a couple of "reds" when the call came for me. "No way do I want to split on this one. I'll be right over."

By the time I arrived at the dealership, the pills had taken effect and I walked through the front door, reached out my hand to the waiting customer, and proceeded to pass out, face-down on the showroom floor.

One of the guys working the showroom floor that morning was kind enough to get me out of there and drive me home. I came back to work the next day and was baffled when I realized my name was taken off the schedule. I had no recall of what had happened the day before, much less that I had been fired. Taylor was there to soothe my wounded ego.

We went out for a drink.

I went on a binge and did not work for a few weeks. Money was running out, and then I had a brainstorm. I contacted a man I had known when I lived in L.A. He had, at one time, offered to set me up in my own business. I had actually become quite good at managing and supervising a telemarketing company. He wanted to set up a boiler room in Orange County and needed someone who knew the inside operations. I called him and within weeks I had a silent partner who backed all the financial aspects of the business. I was now owner and operator of my own business.

I worked long hours—six and seven days a week for the first few months putting the office together, hiring, training, and selling new accounts. Within six months of starting the operation we were turning a profit. I functioned from day to day by drinking, believing that I deserved "a" drink for all the hard work I was doing. Keeping the little airline-sized bottles of alcohol in my top desk drawer, I had a shot of scotch with my morning coffee or with clients. I used cocaine only to relieve my hangovers from the alcohol, and pot to take the edge off the effects I didn't like from the cocaine. Combining drinking and using drugs had become a difficult balancing act.

I often passed out in my car or at the office, or managed to check into a motel. Life became a series of drinking and blackouts, passing out and coming to. I often could not remember what I had done, so I scribbled notes to myself before passing out. This was a trick I had learned in high school. I kept a change of clothes in my car for those mornings when I couldn't make it home the night before.

Joining a gym, I used it as a place to shower in the mornings when I didn't want to face anyone at home or at work before I pulled myself together. In all the time I was a member, the only exercise I got was walking between the gym and my car.

Taylor and I saw very little of each other. We both drank when not working—however, usually not together. We split up many times. I wasn't in love, and I certainly didn't want to get married again. Yet, we were engaged to be married and were buying a house. He wanted to buy a home for the tax breaks, and the only way to get qualified for the loan was to have a second income. The apartment we shared sort of sums up how much we put into the relationship. An ironing board stood for over a year as the only piece of furniture in what was supposed to be the dining area. The TV was sitting on two-by-fours, held up by concrete masonry blocks. We never got around to hanging a single picture on the walls.

The only thing that kept me around was the friendship I had developed with his brother Ryan—he was my drinking buddy. Ryan had just ended a relationship with his girlfriend and showed up at the apartment one Friday night, looking for a place to sleep. He moved in by Monday and the three of us lived together.

Taylor was not home much. But Ryan and I started going out together almost every Sunday morning, hitting just about every champagne brunch in the county that summer.

One morning, we entered a plush restaurant across the street from South Coast Plaza. The maitre d' was almost rude when he explained he didn't have a table and wasn't sure when he would. Ryan and I laughed and said we didn't mind waiting—and went to the bar for a few drinks while we waited.

About every half hour or so, one of us would go check to see if a table had opened up. Each time, the answer was the same: "No, not yet."

After about two hours of waiting we were feeling no pain. I decided that something was not right and that we should both go and talk to this guy to find out what the problem was. Again we were put off.

"No. We do not have a table."

He appeared to be losing his tact. No, he was downright rude.

"What is your problem, buddy?" I questioned loudly.

He replied in his most snobbish tone, "We do not permit people dressed in shorts in our restaurant!"

"Excuse me, sir. You have kept us waiting for over two hours—with no intention of seating us? Ryan, take those shorts off. I'm hungry!"

Ryan began to unzip his pants.

"No! No! Please, sir. Right this way. We do have a table that just opened up!"

He seated us at a small table next to the kitchen doorway.

I enjoyed the occasions we did all get together with Taylor's family. I missed sitting down with a family as I had with the Giaimos.

One of the things that attracted me to Taylor was set in place the night when I was working at the dealership and his mother came in to buy a car. I was impressed with her friendliness and style. She was gorgeous, and Taylor beamed with pride as he introduced Joan to me. The guy liked and was proud of his mother! No one could have guessed she had given birth to and raised six children. Joan glided across the room as though dancing on a ballroom floor. Unfortunately, this attraction was not enough for Taylor and me to build a relationship on.

One of the problems with living with two other drinkers was making sure you had alcohol when you were looking for it. I began hiding my bottle under the kitchen sink, behind the box of Tide. I knew these two guys would never move it to clean. Later, I found out Taylor was hiding his in the toilet tank. No wonder he spent so much time in the bathroom. Other than drinking, Taylor and I had nothing in common. Finally, I couldn't take the arguments and disappointments any longer. We were only hurting one another. I had always met and got involved with guys who had "great potential." I know today that I was certainly no prize myself. It still amazes me how many times I set myself up for disaster.

It never occurred to me to give my telephone number out to some woman I had just met, whether in a bar or elsewhere, because we really enjoyed each other's company. Yet countless times I would give out my telephone number to a total stranger—some man—and then wait for his call. Drinking and using drugs had put me on a collision course for a slow and painful death. At twenty-six years old, I still didn't have a clue about this thing called "life." I wanted out. I wanted to die.

With my head pounding, I was beginning to come around. I forced open my swollen eyes and surveyed the room with blurred vision.

I was alone. The sign on the door told me I was in a motel. What was I doing in a motel again? Fear and humiliation overrode the confusion and pain. Oh God, how I hated myself. If only I had the guts to end it all! Suicide could be no worse than this hell I was putting myself through. My eyeballs were throbbing, and I had a bad case of the jitters. I needed a drink now.

Slowly dragging myself from the bed, I put both feet on the floor and knocked over an empty liquor bottle. Using the nightstand for balance, I stood up. With every part of my body hurting, I had to get something to remedy my suffering. The other side of the room seemed so far away. I staggered to the dresser and found my purse. Searching through it, I found a vial of cocaine and enough pot to roll a joint. I carried cocaine as some might carry aspirin. I didn't use it for getting high. I used it mostly in the morning to cure a hangover. After snorting a line of the white powder, I lit the joint and inhaled deeply. The smoke filled my lungs, quieting my head and steadying my shaking nerves. I had been waking up to this morning ritual for many years. But with the events of this particular morning, I knew I couldn't continue this way.

A car door slammed outside.

Startled, I went to the window just as someone drove away. There was no sign of my car in the parking lot. How did I get here?

I began searching the room, looking for my car keys. "Damn, they must be here."

I dressed and went outside—then wandered around the parking lot, unable to find my car. The panic and fear was mounting. I questioned out loud, "What could have happened to my car?"

As I headed back to the room, the hotel manager approached and eyed me with suspicious curiosity, "Are you all right?"

"Yes!" I snapped and kept moving.

"Are you sure you're okay?" the man probed again.

"I'm fine!" I retorted in a matter-of-fact tone, wishing he would just mind his own business. Then it occurred to me—he could be useful. Maybe he had seen how I arrived there. I toned down the harshness in my voice and haltingly asked him if he knew what had been going on. He was only too eager to give his version.

"Why yes, I did notice you in the car while your gentleman friend signed you both in."

Looking at me more closely he continued, "I also noticed that he had difficulty carrying you up to the room."

Now the guy was making excuses for me. "But, of course, I see that sort of thing from time to time so I didn't pay much attention. Well, that was until I heard the two of you fighting. The other tenants were calling to complain about all the noise. So I called your room. It was about 4 a.m. The next thing I knew, while the telephone was ringing in your room, I saw your friend leaving the room and slamming the door behind him. He drove out of here, tires screeching and all. When I noticed that you were not in the car, I continued to let the phone ring—only to see if you were all right. When you finally answered the phone, you told me to mind my own business and I hung up."

The manager seemed to take some perverse pleasure in telling me the sordid details.

Trying to hide the panic in my voice, I replied, "Well, I wasn't feeling well and needed to get some sleep. Can you tell me what he looked like? Or what kind of car he was driving?"

He described my car.

Alone now and back in the room, I went over to the basin and began splashing cold water on my face. How was I going to get out of this one? I stopped moving for a moment and held my head in my hands. As I lifted my head to the mirror, I recoiled in shock at the image that confronted me. It was the face of my mother.

What was happening to me? I grew up hating alcohol—telling myself I would never end up like my parents. And now, seeing her face in the mirror, I stopped, realizing that so many years had passed and I had become the person I despised most in life.

I forced back the tears and picked up the phone to call my fiancé—well, at least he was the last time I remembered. He agreed to pick me up in a half-hour and hung up.

Sinking back down on the bed, I stared up at the ceiling. "God help me!" This was my first attempt at prayer in many years other than the occasional "God, please get me out of this one. I swear I'll never do it again." I had long before stopped believing in God or religion.

I started to compare my drinking with Taylor's and my mother's. During our three-year relationship, I realized only that he had a drinking problem. He was the one in the bathroom each morning, vomiting into the toilet while running the shower water to disguise the noise.

His bleeding ulcers had become so bad that he mixed vodka with Maalox for breakfast. It couldn't be possible that I also had a drinking problem. I didn't throw up each morning, and I never drank straight from the bottle as my mother did—I always drank from a glass. I continued to deny and justify my own behavior.

My mother-in-law-to-be had gotten sober the year before. Joan had spoken to me several times in the few months prior to this about a program called Al-Anon. I couldn't understand why she wanted to talk to me about getting help. If she thought it was her son who had the drinking problem, why was she speaking to me about a twelve-step program? Overruling my doubts, I made a second call that morning. I asked her to take me to one of those meetings.

When Taylor arrived to pick me up I realized two things: I didn't tell him where I was, and he came in my car. He told me that my behavior was so abusive the night before and that I had, in fact, insisted on being left alone. We had gone out to celebrate Valentine's Day at a comedy nightclub. I left the table and did not return. Concerned about me and annoyed that I had not returned, he asked someone to check the women's bathroom. When this produced no answers, he proceeded to the bar in the next room and found me drinking there. Approaching me, I had rudely told him to "Go away, leave me alone. Can't you see my friend and I want to be alone?" Apparently, I stood there and allowed the guy next to me to hang his arm around my waist and I was kissing the guy. My fiancé walked away and returned to his seat to watch what was left of the show, and to his own drinking. Afterward, he dropped me off at the motel.

Not able to admit my part in this dispute, I had the nerve to get angry at him for leaving me alone. He defended himself, claiming that he wasn't too worried about me because he had my car keys. And, besides, the guy I was with was blind—literally! I had gone to the bar and sat down with a blind comedian.

After he relayed the night's events to me, we drove in silence to his mother's house. I gave up trying to justify my actions.

Taylor never accepted the fact that his mother had a real drinking problem. He believed, and told me, that his mother had joined "another social club" after her twenty-six-year marriage ended.

The first meeting Joan drove me to was beginning. The other newcomers stood up and introduced themselves as "alcoholics." This was an A.A. meeting! Thinking she was taking me to a support group for the families and loved ones of alcoholics, I looked at Joan in total surprise and asked why we were there. I was sure she had taken me to the wrong kind of meeting; she assured me we were in the right place.

Joan was a lifesaver for me. She let me move into her spare bedroom and drove me to meetings each night. Returning to her house after the meetings, she would read a page from a daily meditation book to me and then tucked me into bed. I was scared and confused. No one had ever nurtured me this way. She was one of the first persons who took an active interest in me during my adult life and guided me along, giving lots of love, patience, and gentleness. And she showed little intolerance for the many crazy things I said or did. Joan listened to my never-ending saga of life, as I knew it then. I will always be grateful for her kindness and friendship.

From that moment on, I stopped drinking.

Chapter Fourteen—Facing a New Reality

IN THE FIRST FEW MONTHS OF MY SOBRIETY, I was faced again with unemployment. My silent partner turned out not so silent after we started making a profit with the telemarketing company. He served me with legal documents, trying to gain controlling interest of the business. Fifty-one percent was to be in his favor and three percent in mine, with options for me to earn the balance of my remaining shares over the next five years. I was so angry after battling it out with the attorneys.

I knew I was had. I turned in my keys and company car, and ended our verbal agreement. We were both hurt in the end. I was left with no income. And he, not having the know-how to run it, closed the business.

My engagement ended a few months after I got sober. We both realized the only things we had in common were drinking and his mother.

When things seemed as if they couldn't possibly get any worse, I found the only job opening I was qualified for and went to work for a factory in sales and purchasing. After saving the money for the first and last months' rent, I left Joan's house and moved into an apartment in Huntington Beach. With no transportation for the first time in my life, I took the bus to work each day. I had no furniture and slept on the floor. Each paycheck was carefully managed, and I finally saved up enough to purchase a couch.

I had only been living alone for a few months when my brother contacted me.

Mario was calling from Cleveland. I was so happy to hear from him, it didn't occur to me to ask him why he was calling from a phone booth. He spoke in a low voice and sounded so defeated, explaining that he and his wife of twelve years were separating. He was having a hard time dealing with the separation and needed to get out of town for a while to sort things out. He then asked me if he could please come to California and stay with me. I was so excited, and knew that God was sending me family support. I knew that this must be one of those miracles I had heard about in the twelve-step program. I was clean and sober for almost a month now, and Mario was coming to California to see me!

Mario interrupted my excitement when he informed me he was low on cash and asked if I would mind helping him out. I tried to remain cheerful and replied, "No problem. Go to the airport and I'll have a ticket reserved in your name."

There went the couch money. Instead, I went out that afternoon and purchased two inexpensive twin beds, rationalizing that I could put the two bottom halves together later and add a king size top mattress to it after my brother left.

When Mario walked off the plane at LAX I choked back my shock. We hadn't seen each other in five years and I hadn't anticipated he would look so different—so "Manson-like." I knew about the tattoos, but he also had bandages on his forehead and wrist. He approached me cautiously, looking about the airport even after he saw me. In the car driving back to my apartment, Mario filled me in on more of the sad story of his pending divorce and what was to happen with their three children.

I told Mario briefly about my program to give up alcohol and drugs, and that he could stay with me as long as he didn't bring anything in the way of alcohol or drugs into the apartment. He agreed. He even agreed to try going to a meeting with me.

We attended a twelve-step meeting together the following night. At the meeting, Mario read the popular "twenty questions" that were printed on a single card. After he read through them, I inquired if he identified with any of them.

"No," he replied.

I read one of the questions out loud to him: "Does your family's welfare suffer because of your drinking?"

He responded, "Heck no, my family is still on welfare."

Mario was always a prankster when he was younger, but now he had become devious and deceptive, maliciously betraying people. He believed all of Angelo's lies—that women were the enemy and, therefore, not to be trusted, and that they were only good for one thing.

He actually laughed when he told me the stories about how he tied his wife to the kitchen table before leaving for work so he wouldn't have to worry about her cheating on him. And he laughed about how he killed cats in the neighborhood, running them down with his truck and then driving around the block to make sure they were dead.

He told another story about a group of bikers in the neighborhood who had yelled out obscenities to his wife when she walked or drove by. Mario went after the bikers and plowed into their motorcycles with his car as they stood by or leaned against the bikes.

We talked and stayed together for two weeks. It wasn't enough to cause me to drink, but I was smoking two packs of cigarettes a day and wondering what could possibly happen next.

Mario was making me crazy. Thinking I was living "the good life" out here in California and he could just sit back and enjoy the ride, he became disappointed in me when he found out that he would have to get a job and support himself—that I was living paycheck to paycheck supporting myself. He grew more restless with each passing day.

One night after falling asleep, something unusual happened. I couldn't talk about it to anyone at the time for fear they would call out the "guys in the white coats" and have me put away.

In my dream, I woke in a sudden panic and screamed out, "No, Mario, don't!" I looked toward the bedroom door and saw a black-hooded figure turning his head away from me as he moved through the door. Panicked, I sat straight up in bed and, at that moment, was touched gently on the shoulder. I lay back down, calmed and my fear gone, as the soothing voice of the white figure next to me spoke, "This is all part of the plan." I fell into a deep sleep.

In the morning, I found a note on the kitchen table from Mario. "Sis, I can't take it anymore. I called the Huntington Beach Police Department and turned myself in."

What was going on? Turned himself in . . . for what? I called the police department and verified that they did have a Mario Cicero in custody, pending extradition back to Cleveland. I hung up the phone, and sat down and cried.

I hired him a lawyer in an attempt to postpone his being sent to Ohio. After almost two weeks, the attorney called to give me a full report on Mario's file. First of all, Mario had gotten divorced six months earlier. He then broke into his ex-wife's house and hid in the closet, waiting for her to return. When she came back to the house, she was not alone. She and her boyfriend came in together. Mario waited in the closet for the two of them to go to sleep. The boyfriend went to sleep on the couch, and his ex-wife went into the bedroom and fell asleep. Mario then quietly came out of the closet, crept up on his ex-wife, and pinned her down as he tied and gagged her. He then proceeded into the living room and beat the sleeping boyfriend over the head with a hammer, leaving him for dead, and then he kidnapped her. The report went on to say he was considered extremely dangerous, schizophrenic.

I was sick. Not only was all this happening, but I had been harboring a criminal. I had helped him escape from Ohio. His call to me for help came from a phone booth after escaping from a mental ward for the criminally insane.

I was forced to let go; Mario was on his own. He was transferred from Orange County jail and flown back to Cleveland.

On the rebound from the breakup with Taylor and now being sober for a year, my boss at the factory introduced me to my soon-to-be second husband, Darryl. I believed he was God's will for me since we had not met in a bar. We dated only a few weeks before moving in together, and then lived together for a few months before leaving for Vegas on a Sunday night.

One of the problems with not planning ahead to get married is not knowing what to wear, and no time or money to buy something new.

For the first "wedding" in 1974, I was dressed in a purple halter-top dress. Now, eight years later, I pulled a red silk dress from the closet.

Getting married sounded like a good idea at the time—at least it was more appealing than going to work on Monday morning. We never discussed much of anything. Darryl knew that I didn't drink, and I had to go to those meetings. I knew he had two sons from his first marriage. And when they came to visit, I went out shopping.

Only four days after we were married, he came home drunk and proceeded to drink on a daily basis. Darryl practically lived in the garage, tinkering with an old Chevy truck while drinking beer from the refrigerator he kept in the garage. Our neighbor kept him company. We jokingly referred to him as the "walking six-pack." He arrived each night with a can of beer, one in each of the two back pockets, and one in each of the two front pockets of his oversized work pants. The pants hung down below his beer gut. He carried the other two cans, one in each hand.

Darryl quit his job within a month or so. For a while, he left the house each day pretending to be going off to work. His ex-wife delivered one of the two boys from his first marriage to the house, reporting that she couldn't control him. And as if this wasn't enough, my cigarette-sharing spouse gave up smoking and took up chewing. We stopped kissing from that day forth. He refused to give up using his mouth as an ashtray.

I now had a seven-year-old stepson living with us who resented me, and treated me as I had treated people when I was his age. A five-year-old stepson showed up every other weekend to stay with us. Living forty miles away from where I worked, I was driving three or four hours every day depending on the freeway traffic.

I knew only months into the marriage that it was a horrible mistake. Ashamed and embarrassed to let anyone know, I kept quiet about how miserable we were together. I took some of the messages I had learned in the program and ended up beating myself up over them—things like "Keep your eyes on yourself," and "Take your own inventory." I wanted to believe that God was going to swoop down one day and zap our marriage, and "they would live happily ever after."

I prayed. I went to A.A. meetings. I worked full time and took care of his children. He stopped talking to me one day. For three days we lived in total silence. I was stunned at first, not knowing what I had done to possibly upset him. I was too tired and too fed up at the time to pursue asking him why he was not talking to me. I flipped in and out of anger. "He can go to hell. I don't want to talk to him anyway!"

On the third day, we sat across the table from each other eating the meal I had prepared for him and his son. When we finished dinner, I sent the son out to play with his friends. I finally asked calmly, "What is the matter?" No response. Again, I questioned him, "Why won't you tell me what is wrong? How long do you plan on not talking to me?" He responded in a very low and slow manner of speaking. "Well, it really bothers me that you leave the dishes in the sink sometimes at night—and my ex-wife never did that."

I looked at him in disbelief. I drew in a deep breath and exhaled to calm myself before responding. The program had taught me that resentment was our number one killer. So I answered with a deliberate, slow, and low tone in my voice. "Let me see if I've got this right. You haven't spoken to me for three days now because your ex-wife never left dishes in the sink?"

And then something in me snapped. I went into a rage. My voice rose higher than it had ever gone before as I added, "IF YOU DON'T LIKE THE DISHES IN THE SINK, GET OFF YOUR BUTT AND WASH THEM. AND IF YOUR EX-WIFE IS SUCH A SAINT, WHY ARE YOU TWO DIVORCED?"

We never discussed her or the dishes again. Each night after I prepared dinner, he got up and did the dishes.

I flew to Cleveland after hearing my father was dying of cancer. My first reaction was disbelief. Not trusting the information from my brother, I called the hospital to see if they had Angelo Cicero listed as a patient. After explaining that I was his daughter and lived in California, they agreed to let me speak to his doctor. The doctor confirmed the story and said he was sorry to say he only had a matter of weeks to live.

I was not sure if it was an excuse for me to get away from the home life for a few days, or if I really wanted to see my father one more time before he died.

He was on morphine for the pain when I arrived. It was a shock for me to see how much he had deteriorated. The once handsome and proud man weighed about seventy-five pounds. Unable to speak, he nodded toward me, then turned and walked away to sit on the front porch. My life of "do as you're told" flashed before me as I sat down and cried. The anger and pain surfaced—all the mind-games he had played. All the cons and victimizing couldn't save him from this ending.

Why did I still have so many emotions for this man? I loathed him. I wanted to scream out, "Damn you! You did this to yourself, you bastard!" But I was not about to admit to him or myself that any part of me still wanted "daddy's" acceptance and approval. I silenced my voice. I knew that in the Cicero family there was no respect shown for anyone. I had watched them play with others' emotions all of my life, making fun of everything and everyone.

I sat in the house and looked out the window at Angelo, who sat hunched over in a chair on the porch. Tears filled my eyes. The dam broke. I began sobbing. I allowed myself to feel a wide range of emotions. In the end I was able to let go. There were no more tears to cry. I was experiencing firsthand what happens to the alcoholic drug addict. I did not want my life to end as his was ending.

Returning to California the same day, I left without talking to or seeing anyone else.

Angelo weighed sixty-five pounds when he died two months later. I did not attend his funeral.

My marriage lasted less than two years. I left my second husband after his "true confession." He came home one evening and informed me that he couldn't live "the lie" anymore. We spent hours that evening as he gave his report of all the woes of his childhood. I sat listening attentively, until he informed me that he was currently having an affair. I knew we had many problems in our relationship, but I had no idea this was one of them!

I went to bed that night and the following night, pretending all was well. I continued my daily routine the same as always, driving my stepson to school and going in to work. Two days later at work, I was on the telephone with a customer when my hand began to shake. I couldn't imagine what was causing it. Nothing like this had ever happened to me before. Now, both hands were shaking. I quickly excused myself and hung up the telephone. The shaking was getting worse. I didn't know what was happening to me, but I knew I didn't want it to happen at work. I grabbed my purse from under the desk, pushed my chair back, and ran down the hall. My legs felt weak as I moved to escape. The bookkeeper heard my chair fall backwards and made it to her doorway by the time I went racing by. She called out to me, but I kept running until I got to my car.

I wanted to scream but couldn't, and gripped tightly to the steering wheel as I drove away. I had no idea what I was doing or where I was going. I just kept driving.

Over the next month, I did not return home. I checked into hotels from L.A. to Orange County, and I stayed with a woman friend named Genny Baker and other friends in the program. I was devastated. How could I have made such a colossal mistake? I blamed no one but myself. My health was deteriorating, and I was on a steady diet of coffee and two-plus packs of cigarettes a day. Not able to eat, I lost twenty pounds and went from a size twelve to a size six.

I had no other choice but to move into someone else's house, and rented a room from Genny. She was very kind and generous toward me. However, even after months of living with her, my emotional state had not recovered. In fact, it was becoming more difficult to hide my depression from her and others.

The shock and betrayal of my husband's confession still haunted me. And now I was hanging on only by a thread. I did my best to go in to work on most days during the first few months of the separation, pending my divorce. The most difficult thing I faced at that moment was losing the relationship with the stepchildren. I had grown to love them. They didn't deserve having someone walk out on them without an explanation.

Others tried to comfort me, telling me "They're not your children, and not your problem."

But the pain did not lessen. As an ex-step-parent, you have no visitation rights. Mr. Metz felt badly that he had introduced me to Darryl. He held my position for me as I slowly tried to piece my life back together.

Two months after my separation, I received a telephone call one morning from Jack Conway, informing me about his wife's death.

My foster mother, Judy, had been suffering from and fighting lung cancer for the past six months, and had died only a few hours earlier.

I made reservations to leave for Cleveland the following day. I was too numb to feel the loss for Jack and his children, but felt I should go to the funeral. I tossed and turned that night, trying to sleep.

About ten-thirty, I received yet another telephone call. This time it was Becky, my sister-in-law. There was an eerie calmness about her as she told me my brother was dead. She hesitated only briefly when I asked how it had happened. I was stunned when she said he had taken his own life. He had gone in to take a shower, and when he didn't come out almost an hour later she went in and found him. He was hanging from the shower faucet with a belt tied around his neck. Tony was only thirty-eight years old.

I canceled my trip to Cleveland and missed the services for Judy. I needed to be in California to help Becky get Tony buried. Becky did not even have the money to bury her husband.

I drove with Becky to make the arrangements for his burial services at March Air Force Base. She decided not to hold any services in a funeral home, but she did want to go and see her dead husband one more time before he was to be cremated. She said she wanted him cremated to make sure he couldn't come back.

Not being prepared for it, I was mortified when they wheeled him out on a gurney in a plastic bag. I really hadn't given it much thought prior to seeing him. The guy who worked at the base said no words and showed no emotions as he unzipped the bag, exposing Tony's face. I looked at his face for a few seconds before turning away. Yes, he was dead. And I was hit with anger, not sadness. "Good, the bastard's gone," I thought to myself.

The next day I drove out to pick Becky up and drive her back out to the base for the burial. A military man, dressed in uniform, read from an index card: "We are all gathered here today . . . " Following this, another man in uniform pulled a tape recorder from his pocket and played "Taps." Becky, her parents, and I—along with the two guys from the military—were the only people who attended his services. Tony had used up all his contacts with the family, and the only friend he had left when he died moved in with his wife before the ashes were cold.

I had my suspicions about Tony's suicide, believing that it was masochistic tendencies that led to his death. He didn't have it in him to kill himself. Unable to do himself harm, he was obsessed, instead, with provoking others into doing it for him. Only months after his apparent suicide, I heard the worst news of all. He had been sexually abusing his nine-year-old daughter.

Soon after this, I learned about autoerotic-asphyxiation, where people get sexual pleasure from choking themselves while masturbating. And the pieces fit into place.

This would have been more like the Tony I knew.

Chapter Fifteen—The Unknowable

AT THIRTY-ONE, I wanted to die more than I wanted to live. Crumbling under the despair of problems, I couldn't cope with myself and I didn't want to be around anyone. Being married and divorced twice, no family to turn to, and with a job I was just getting by on, everything seemed unbearable.

With my health deteriorating, I was seeing a doctor for depression and internal bleeding. I started, under protest, to see a therapist, Donna Kopp. On the days that I did force myself out of bed to get to the office, I functioned as a robot with frequent "short circuiting." I was splitting off from moment to moment. Keeping focused and living in the here and now was less appealing to me.

I had been dry for four years and had not yet been able to face looking at myself, face my past, or accept life on life's terms. I had been hearing this message, and yet death began to look more appealing to me as the only way out of my pain. I was trying to cope with learning how to live alone and without the aid of booze or pills for the first time in my life—fighting daily just to do the basics. My weight was way down and I continued to smoke two packs of cigarettes a day.

Finally, I woke one morning and I found myself planning my own death. I was exhausted. Nothing seemed to be working. Life was just not worth living. I tried to get out of bed and fell to the floor. Other than forcing down a cracker or two, I had not eaten in a few days. I lay on the floor, trying to figure out how to speed up the process. I knew I was going to die eventually if I didn't start eating and quit smoking. But I realized that killing myself this way was going to be a very long, dragged out process.

My mind was working slowly as I tried to think what I might have in the apartment to move things along more quickly. I didn't even have aspirins in the place. Besides, I had heard that most people throw up after swallowing handfuls of them, and the technique rarely worked. Next, I thought about a razor blade but wondered if my BIC disposable blade would cut deep enough. Frustrated, I just couldn't come up with a solution, so I crawled over to the nightstand and picked up the telephone.

Donna answered the phone after only one ring. I broke down in sobs, "I can't do this anymore!"

She calmly asked me, "What can't you do?"

I suspected she was trying to keep me on the phone. "I don't want to live," I burst out through the sobbing.

Donna patiently explained more about depression. I had been seeing her for months now, and I still wanted to die more than I wanted to live. But I was too exhausted to hang up on her and it wouldn't be polite. So I continued to listen to her about how I needed to force myself to do something physical, anything just to get my body moving. She went on to say that if we didn't work depression out, it would eat in on me.

"Sandy, you have to move your body," she continued.

Speaking at a barely audible volume, I responded: "I can't. I am so tired."

"Do something—anything. Turn on some music. Begin by moving your arms or dancing."

Now I was questioning her sanity. Was she kidding, dancing? I couldn't get up off the floor and she was telling me to dance. But I held the receiver and listened on. After all, I was now a sober people-pleaser.

"Yes, I'm still here," I replied. Donna had another idea and asked me if there was a swimming pool at the apartment complex. She instructed me to go and try swimming one lap or just try floating. I was to return from this outing and call her back. She would be waiting for my call. I thanked her for her help, hung up the phone, and thought: What an idiot! She doesn't get it! No one understands. I just don't give a damn. I don't have the energy to go for a swim.

My thoughts were interrupted by the ringing of the telephone. My fingers had not left the telephone and were still on the receiver. Hesitating for another ring, I picked up the phone and put it to my ear. It was Donna calling me back. "Sandy, you can swim, can't you?" she blurted out.

With that I burst into laughter. Here I was trying to figure out how to kill myself, and when I called for help I received the perfect answer—go drown yourself. God, indeed, works in mysterious ways. But the laughter broke the spell I was in at the time and the thought of committing suicide passed.

Living one day at a time—sometimes one minute at a time—sustained me through my nightmare. I continued with the counseling and started keeping a journal—looking at what I wanted from life for the first time. Before that, I had never sat down and given any time to thinking about tomorrow, next week, or next year. I never had a clue how to do this.

In therapy, I recalled each time a brick had gone into building the wall that I hid behind for years. I remembered crying out—no one cared; another brick was set in place. I was giving up and losing all hope as the walls closed in. I crawled into the corner somewhere deep inside. They built my wall. I was the prisoner—they were gone.

With the constant support of my therapist and the many wonderful friends in the program, I slowly began to remove each brick, one at a time.

So many events have led me to the person I am today. Through my involvement with A.A., I have met some terrific people. It was so difficult in the beginning. I sat in those meetings, crying, angry and confused. I was filled with the "yeah buts." I felt so different and unique. But I was encouraged to "just keep coming back"—no matter what.

I, once again, had to learn a whole new lingo. The verbiage and slogans drove me crazy. There were times when I thought I would scream if I heard one more time, "This too shall pass."

When my first A.A. meeting ended, we all stood in a circle and held our hands together while reciting "The Lord's Prayer"; I wanted to run to get as far away from God, or anyone who preached God, as I could. The Twelve Steps suggested "God as we understood him." Well, this was not an easy task. I understood God all right—He was mean and vengeful. "Vengeance is mine, saith the Lord," I had heard all my life about this vengeful God. But the support I received back was "Take what you want and leave the rest."

After much whining on my part, I even heard "There are only two things you need to know about God. One, there is a God. And two, it's not you!"

Learning to trust, to pray, and finally to meditate came very slowly for me. When I first started attending meetings, I hated being there. I thought I would jump out of my skin just sitting in the chair. But I saw hope in those rooms. I heard others talk about things that I, too, had felt but never told another human being. I started to feel a part of for the first time in my life.

I've learned to stay away from the people in the program that use it only as a "dumping ground," and follow the advice of "carry the message, not the mess."

I also believe that A.A. is not the bedrock of mental health. We do need to pray and meditate to learn discernment and sound judgment, so as not to be manipulated by those who choose to stay sick. One of the many lessons I've come to learn is that some people want to stay sick more than they want to get well. The program is for those who want it, not for those who need it.

At times, it was absolutely maddening to get a question answered—ask fifteen people, and you'll get fifteen different responses or opinions. Even when I didn't ask, I still got others' opinions.

Today, we are faced with a lot of controversy, but so is the whole world. Controversies have pushed me into taking a stand. Before I got sober, I never took a stand. If I had an opinion on something, I never let you know what it was.

I had lost my voice as a child, always being silenced one way or another. I became a "people pleaser" until I started to drink.

Drinking allowed me to have a voice—an angry and belligerent one. After a few years in recovery, I learned to recognize when I was being a "people pleaser"—and learned how to speak up.

It has been said, "all it takes is a resentment and a coffee pot to start a new meeting." We have even joked about some characters in the program who have single-handedly been responsible for starting more meetings than anyone else, because people got so upset with their actions that they went off and started new meetings.

But this is the greatest "school" I have ever found. I get to learn how to trust my God-given instincts, to fall and get up again. With all the trials I have endured, and all the errors I've made over the years, I have not had to walk through any of them alone—unless I chose to. This is only one path in many. I will be forever grateful to the folks who, like myself, continue to keep coming back to give back what was there for me and so many others—all for a few dollars in the basket.

I can look in the mirror today and say I like myself—just as I am. I can laugh today! Through many different processes—returning to school, reading many self-help or inspirational books, and seeking outside professional help—I have learned to love and to forgive; forgiveness of others, and of myself. One of the many slogans that used to drive me crazy, and now I can appreciate, is "EGO" means "easing God out."

When Life magazine came out with a fiftieth anniversary edition, I was willing and able to detach from my life, and see that the world out there can be enormous or small. In seeing the various dates of events in history, I was able to piece together how old I was at a particular event in time. The year Kennedy was shot, I was in the orphanage at nine years old. Later, I found some of the pieces of the puzzle to my life by taking an American history class on the sixties in junior college.

Younger students in the class made remarks about my age, and wanted to know why I was studying the sixties. "Didn't you live it?" they questioned.

"Yes, I did live it. That's why I am here!" I replied.

Listening to others, in groups and individually, I began to understand feelings—my own and others'. I stopped looking for the differences—and began looking for the similarities or feelings in others. I discovered I am not so unique—we are all the same.

Chapter Sixteen—Third Time's the Charm

AT THIRTY-TWO YEARS OLD I had made up my mind that relationships were just not meant to be for me. I have heard others in A.A. say, "They may have another drunk left in them, but they don't have another recovery."

My motto had become, "I may have another man or relationship—but I do not have another recovery!"

One day, I finally decided to take an inventory of the men in my life. Sitting down as suggested with a pad of paper, I drew three columns on it. In the first, I listed all the names of any male that came to mind. The instructions were to list all males (father, brothers, grandfathers, uncles, teachers, and kids from the neighborhood or school). What an order!

But I did it. I was sick and tired of being sick and tired. Now, in the second column I was to list one word to describe each person. And, in the final column what I received from each. Upon completion I was amazed. Through it I was able to see my own patterns. I could see why my now adult relationships kept failing—why I kept being drawn to the same type of man; how I kept doing the same thing over and over, expecting different results. Through this I have learned what it means, "To thine own self be true."

I have stopped being the victim.

I now communicate my needs to others. If they are not able to accept me for who I am, I do not accept them into my life. I reached a point of honesty and self-love, knowing that I could for the first time in my life live alone and be happy.

Joan is still my sponsor and friend. After about a year of learning about myself and changing the things that no longer served me in a positive way, I started dating again. After a few more failed attempts, Joan invited me to go to a meeting with her. She would not admit until much later that she invited me there to introduce me to someone.

Jeff was tall and handsome. He was quiet, college educated, owned a house, worked for the same company for over fifteen years, and was sober for five years.

Joan had given him my phone number.

Jeff called and invited me out to dinner. He was so sincere when he responded to my acceptance, "YOU WILL?" I had to laugh.

For the first time in my life I began asking questions before considering marriage. We dated for six months and did not live together. I had my doubts about him at first and mentioned to my therapist and Joan, "He isn't like any guy I've dated before."

Joan and Donna were happy to hear this. "This is a good thing, Sandy."

Jeff proposed to me in Yosemite National Park on a trip we had taken together. I was really engaged for the first time, and we got married on the anniversary of our first date. This year we celebrated eight years of marriage. We have grown closer to each other spiritually, and continue to grow individually and as a couple.

With each passing day, I truly believe God gave me another chance. I have been able to accomplish so many things in my life today, and I am deeply grateful for the love and support that Jeff continues to show me each day.

Jeff and I agreed that if we had met earlier in our lives perhaps we could have wanted children, but with my family heritage we decided not to take any chances. Our friends would come over to the house, always with the same message: "Your home is beautiful. But, it's so quiet here!"

We like quiet. We enjoy our freedom.

Then one day, after eight glorious years of happy and quiet bliss, Jeff came home with a puppy for my birthday. He was the cutest puppy in the whole world. No really, he was. Everyone who came over to the house said so.

Friends kept coming, two or three different times a day for almost a month. They all said the same thing. "Oh, he's so cute! And I had to come over when I heard you have a dog. I can't believe it!"

Well the puppy is now fifteen months old. Those same people now say, "Why don't you take him to obedience school?"

We reply with, "We don't have a problem with an eighty-pound lap dog. We like our puppy just the way he is." Okay, maybe he is a "dog," but he still likes being referred to as "the kid," or "Willie puppy."

Our home is filled with warmth and love. We both enjoy and appreciate antiques and have surrounded ourselves with a few we have collected over the years. Grandma Cicero influenced my taste in deep, richly-colored mahogany woods. I also have a wonderful overstuffed chair with a matching footstool. Propped snuggling into its cushions, at times I can close my eyes and feel her with me.

Studying at night, I earned my high school General Education Diploma. For the Ciceros in my immediate family, a high school diploma is a big deal. I was finally able to take college courses, and made the Dean's List while receiving a Certificate of Achievement in Human Services.

Jeff and I took a trip to Eugene, Oregon two summers ago. I never thought I would see Eugene again. It had an amazing effect on me when we first arrived. Jeff held my hand as we walked through the town. A part of me over the years wondered if it ever really existed. Overcome with emotion, seeing it again after twenty years, I was able to say, "It is real. And it does exist." We checked into a motel and went driving around the town. The house that used to be on 1010 High Street had been moved and relocated to another street, and was being restored to its original condition.

Next, we went to the local newspaper and spoke to a reporter who worked for the paper during the early seventies. He was kind enough to print out a few articles that had been written years earlier about Shiloh. I was pleased to obtain copies. It confirmed that I had indeed made the right decision to leave Shiloh—that I was not wicked or wrong in my suspicions. The newspaper articles stated the IRS had been investigating its leaders for tax evasion.

Shiloh had manipulated its followers through fear: "God will get you if you don't be good—if you don't follow our way."

The message was pretty much the same as in Parmadale. Only, once again, this group believed their way was the only way. We gave up our free will.

Like many of the different paths I have followed in my life, I seem to get caught up in the "They must know better than I." But eventually my intuition or gut feelings keep coming back, and my head won't stop until I take the appropriate action. When I start to get a gut feeling that something is wrong, and I can't stop the confusion in my head, when I can't make a decision without checking in with someone else, I know I am in trouble. I don't believe that my Higher Power, whom I choose to call God, is one of confusion—but rather of peace and serenity. For me God is love. Love is God. I heard a member in a twelve-step program speak. He said: "We have all heard if you take a drunken horse thief and sober him up you still have a horse thief." But he went on to say: "It doesn't matter if you are a horse thief, it doesn't matter how many horses you stole . . . What matters is why." I continue to look within myself to let go of all the whys.

Lynn McClure and I have since talked fondly of our days in the commune. It was exciting to be a part of something so outrageous in the sixties. We laugh at ourselves and the things we did. Like most teenagers, we rebelled against the strict supervision of those who served in the name of the Lord. She, too, snuck out and ventured about on her own as often as possible—only to return to the scornful reprimands of the elders. We both knew nothing of cults back then, and only saw this as a safe haven from the streets and drugs. Jacque insisted that Lynn was to leave Shiloh and return home after Lynn informed her that she was asked to turn over the pink slip on her car.

The coincidences over the next few days were exciting.

When I mentioned our reason for being in Eugene to the woman who worked behind the desk of the motel, she spoke up about her own involvement and disappointments with Shiloh.

With no idea of The Land's exact location, Jeff and I drove forty miles out to Dexter. We stopped for sodas at a small market in the country. As Jeff paid for the sodas, I noticed a woman who was sweeping the floor in the back of the store and intuitively asked her if she had ever heard of a group that was around twenty years ago and called themselves "Shiloh."

She smiled. "Now that's a name I haven't heard mentioned in a while. Why, yes, I did know of them. They owned some property outside of town but the last I heard they sold it." After I questioned her about its location, she vaguely explained how to get there. "Well, I don't know for sure where it is, but if you follow this road out in front and . . . it's somewhere out there."

Grinning, Jeff and I returned to the car. Yes, it's here somewhere.

We drove about another half-hour into a heavily wooded area and passed a narrow dirt and gravel road on our left. I mumbled to Jeff, "I think that's it."

My tone of voice did not convince him. So we continued on the road only a short distance. Finally I demanded, "No, turn around. I know that's it." It was.

Driving slowly down the rough, tree-lined road, we came to a clearing after about a quarter of a mile and pulled to a stop in front of the shack-like cabins that were still standing after twenty years. The Land looked the same, and the woods were just as serene as they had been back then. I did have some fond memories of this place. The pines were taller and the energy was wonderful.

A woman was playing with a few small children in front of the old dining lodge. We got out of the car and introduced ourselves to the few adults who greeted us. At first, they seemed suspicious and uneasy about our intrusion. The tension disappeared after I introduced myself and Jeff, and explained to them that the purpose of the visit was to show my husband the place where I had once lived—that I was once a member of the Shiloh group that had originally owned the property and built these very cabins.

In awe, one of the young women reacted, "You lived here?"

She relaxed and explained what they were doing there. It was more than a flashback—it was history repeating itself.

This group of men, women, and their families had recently bought the property from Shiloh and boasted about how they wanted to return to nature and live as organically as possible, living off the land and growing all their own vegetables. To them, this had to be a new concept. They seemed disappointed when I responded with a smile, saying that's what we had done in the late sixties.

Not wanting to hear any more from me, one of the women turned to play once more with the children. Hoping not to impose on them, I gently asked if we could walk around and take a few pictures. It was great to see this place again. When I was younger, I appreciated the beauty of the surroundings and spent many afternoons after my chores were complete walking through the woods. But I didn't realize at the time all the work and skill that went into building it.

The sun was starting to set. I had seen what I came to see. Jokingly, I whispered to Jeff, "We should not wander too far from the car. Who knows what this group believes. How do we know it's not another Jim Jones setup?"

Waking early the following morning, we had one more stop to make—the high school where I hoped to see or get a copy of my school records. I still could not remember how old I was, or even what year I had lived in Eugene. The years between sixteen and twenty-six were still only vague memories. Now, because of this visit another piece of the puzzle had been solved. I did obtain a copy of my school records showing that I had attended South Eugene High in 1972. Another ghost of my past was released.

We left Eugene after three days, leaving behind the shame and guilt I had carried since my decision to escape from the Shiloh ministry. In my life I had been baptized as a Catholic without my consent, a Christian twice, a Baptist once, and it wasn't until I was baptized in alcohol that I was brought to my knees.

By changing my belief systems, I have been able to see how far I have come in my life and how far I have yet to go. It has taken many years to get to know myself fully. Through prayer and meditation, I am learning how to access the spirit of God in me—in each of us. We are spiritual beings first and human beings second. Pain is the price we pay for forgetting our spiritual origins. As it has been said "there is nothing new under the sun."

Today I know this to be true—adding "only my awareness and acceptance is new."   I have so much gratitude for all those who had been willing to go before me, and who are now showing others the way.

As for my family…

Chapter Seventeen—The Boys

Drifter

BASEBALL, FOOTBALL, RUNNING AND SINGING Elvis songs kept Albert going—that and sneaking drugs from Dad and selling them to the kids in the neighborhood. He never finished any sort of formal education, dropping out of school in the fifth grade.

Faced with going to court, he changed his birth certificate to show he was sixteen rather than fifteen. He went face-to-face with the judge, who gave him an ultimatum: "You have two choices, jail or the army."

Albert joined the army.

After his tour of duty in Vietnam, Albert returned to Cleveland. He was still impulsive, infantile, and obnoxious. Following in Dad's footsteps, he met a thirteen-year-old girl in the neighborhood and got her pregnant. Later, they got married and their daughter was born.

Albert worked odd jobs on and off, mostly off. His drinking and drugs came first. After two years, his wife heard that while she was out working and trying to support them, Albert was sleeping with the local "door knocker" who came to preach Jehovah. Hurt, angry, and fifteen years old with a child, the wife wised up and divorced him.

It didn't take the Jehovah woman long to walk down the aisle with her new convert. After all, she had three children at home from her first marriage who needed food. Soon after the "I do's," wife number two gave birth to Albert's second daughter. The Jehovah didn't take kindly to Albert's first daughter and managed to convince him to turn his back on her.

Albert stayed home and didn't bother to work. He continued to drink and take drugs when this wife was out. She earned her living by cleaning houses, finding work through the church. When not working, and with her other daughters in school, she dragged their daughter door to door and preached Jehovah to all who would listen. At least the stepchildren had their real father to return to—and they did as soon as they were old enough to get out of the house.

I was livid to learn from my niece—the child from Albert's first marriage—that she is not permitted to address her father as "Dad," and has been instructed to call him by his first name only. She is heartbroken, confused, and angry—wondering why she has been treated as an outcast. On the rare occasion that he does decide to appear unannounced in her life, he pretends that nothing has happened.

Three generations after Angelo, another child is born. How will she be told about her family heritage? How will she understand that her grandfather, Albert, who lives in the same city, has little contact with her or her family?

Inmate

GONE IS THE EIGHT-YEAR-OLD COMIC who could make me laugh. Mario was the only one of my brothers who helped me around the house with the chores, even though as Angelo considered it to be "girl's work."

Like his dad, though, he had a temper, and when it flared up you didn't want to be on the receiving end of it. A schoolteacher called him to the front of the room to scold him for disrupting the class. When Mario smirked and smarted off to the teacher, the teacher slapped him upside the head and messed up Mario's hair. Mario took great pride in his appearance, and in slicking down every hair into place with Vitalis. Mario went into a rage and punched the teacher in the face. He was suspended from school.

Mario was discharged from the army after being AWOL several times. In between his going in and out of prison, his wife gave birth to three children.

Mario just couldn't seem to stay out of jail. The crimes became worse and the sentences longer. Returned to prison for the third time, he is currently serving a twelve- to twenty-five year sentence for kidnapping and attempted manslaughter. I stopped all contact with him over eight years ago. His letters became so twisted and evil that they became too painful for me to read. Mario believes he is the second coming of Christ, or rather he says "Christ's brother"—here to pick up where Jesus left off. He believes everything he does is directed by God. In one of his last letters, he informed me that God had spoken to him and shared a special message: "Dandelions are the cure for AIDS." I haven't informed medical science of this yet!

At twenty-seven, Mario worshipped his father and wanted to go to college. He had heard the stories told so many times about life on the inside. As Angelo spun his web of deceit, he even made prison sound attractive. Mario wanted to prove he was every bit the man that Angelo was. He wanted his daddy's approval. Angelo sent cigarettes and coffee to him in prison. Mario went down with the ultimate betrayal. Angelo died.

His ex-wife abandoned the three children and went into hiding after Mario was sent back to prison. She has not been seen or heard from since. The two daughters ended up living in different foster homes, and his son was raised by an aunt.

One of the daughters ended up living with Amy and her husband. With alcoholism being a progressive problem, I can only imagine what this child has endured living with two practicing alcoholics. The arrangements for her to live with them were approved by the same court system that took Amy's children away from her years earlier.

History continues to repeat itself. Angelo was in prison when his father died; Mario was in prison when Angelo died. And now the parole board says Mario is ready to return to society. Mario has been isolated from reality since he was eight years old.

I pray for the children he left behind—who were only seven, eight, and ten years old when he went into prison—and his ex-wife. The three children have struggled along in life and are now in their early twenties. They have had little or no contact with their father or mother.

Amy and Johnny reach into their pockets and send Mario a few bucks each month in prison. Amy had the gall to brag about how much "Mario is enjoying the new prison he was relocated to—he gets popcorn and a movie on Friday nights."

I came unglued with this one. "And this makes you feel like Mother Theresa because your forty-two-year-old son is happy with popcorn and a movie on Friday nights?"

Gambler

SAM AND I HAVE NOT BEEN CLOSE. On the few trips I made to Cleveland to attend family funerals, Sam and I met only briefly to see one another. But too much time had passed between conversations. We were polite with each other, but nothing of any importance was spoken. Just as I had done for so many years, Sam hides behind his own brick wall.

Yet, I continue to hold a place in my heart for him. Sam is, underneath it all, probably more like me than we will ever know. He was sensitive, artistic, and cried easily. Unfortunately, no one ever trained or encouraged him to pursue art.

When the boys and I sat down to play cards as children, Sam cried out each time, "You guys are cheating!"

We were, but never admitted it.

He was the youngest in the family and followed his big brothers around until he found an identity for himself as a gambler and biker. He was passionate and good at both.

Sam had been angry at Angelo and had not seen him for over a year. Uncle Ozzie contacted him, pleading with him to "Go and see your father before he dies." I tried and yet Sam held out, refusing to let others dictate to him what he was or was not going to do. He finally gave in and went to see Angelo at Holy Cross Cancer Home. Angelo died later that day.

Sam managed to stay out of military service and jail. Rumor had it that he was involved with Mario on a couple of "jobs," but Mario took the rap for both—leaving Sam to marry and have two daughters.

I held a lot of hope for him. Sam was the only brother who managed to hold onto the same job for any length of time. But after ten years on the job he cashed in his pension, blew most of the money on a Harley Davidson motorcycle, and paid off some of his gambling debts with what was left. His wife and children were crushed. He had promised them for two years that when he got that money they would buy a home and move out of the apartment, buy a new car, and drive to California to see Disneyland and me. None of these grandiose promises ever materialized.

I was furious with him when I witnessed him mocking and making fun of his fifteen-year-old daughter for crying—another family tradition living on. He was treating her just as he had been treated. Crying or showing emotions were not tolerated in the Cicero family. He snapped at her, yelling that she was just like her mother. These very words—the same words I had heard so many times from Angelo. It shocked and saddened me to hear my brother acting the same way with his children. I jumped in to intervene. "Sam, don't you dare speak to your daughter this way!" He snapped back at me and told me to mind my own business. That was over four years ago, and the last time I saw him.

On February 14th, 2003, Sam was returning home from hanging out with his friends at the bar. His Harley was hit head-on by a van. He suffered a severe head trauma and died before morning. He was forty-six years old.

With no insurance or money to pay for a funeral, Sam's friends and family rallied together at the bar and, passing a basket, managed to collect six thousand dollars to pay for his services.

Chapter Eighteen—It's Not a Love Story

AMY CONTINUES TO PLAY the victim role and is absolutely maddening. She attempts to manipulate by playing "he said, she said" with her children and grandchildren. And as a bingo runner for the local Catholic church on Thursday nights, the tips keep a supply of drinking money coming in.

She complains about her husband of over twenty years, that he is so tight he squeaks. "He'll only buy me one bottle of whiskey on Friday night, and expects this to last me all week!" He pays for her drinking in a bar from Friday through Sunday, but that doesn't count.

Two years ago, Amy called to inform me she was going to Las Vegas. The Copper Penny was located across the street from the five hundred square foot house where she has lived for twenty years. The thought of the owner closing the bar so he could go on vacation caused an uproar from its patrons—her "friends." They came up with the brilliant idea that they should all go on one of those "party flights" together.

I took the bait and agreed to meet her in Vegas, convincing myself this might be the last time I would see her alive. Amy had been in poor health for several years—her liver was enlarged, and one kidney had been removed. She complained often about her many trips to the hospital emergency room to have urine pumped from her system. The blame for her improperly working bladder was always "what your father did to me."

My second rationalization for going was that I couldn't resist seeing Amy in some environment other than the neighborhood. Her husband, Johnny, worked many hours in a factory, doing manual labor, and retired after thirty-five years on the same job. He had purchased their house for six thousand dollars soon after they were married. Johnny has worked hard his whole life and seems to take pride in taking care of Amy. And now my mother was leaving the neighborhood for the first time in over forty years (other than the car trips to Pennsylvania). I had never seen my mother in any other setting, and could not believe what I was hearing. She was actually going to get on an airplane.

I arranged to drive to Vegas with a couple of girlfriends.

Amy had told me she would be staying at the Imperial Casino. I don't know why I even bothered to go to her room first. I should have known I would find her sitting at the bar. My very first thought on seeing her was, "So much for seeing her in a different environment!"

Amy didn't bother to get up when I walked up to her. I was hurt to see her "being herself."

Why do I keep setting myself up, thinking things will be different with her? We do not show emotions; how could I keep forgetting this? So what if I drove from California to Vegas to see her. Did this entitle me to a hug? I mean really, Sandy, you just saw her two years ago in Cleveland.

My head continued to inventory the situation. Amy sat there, playing the video poker machine in front of her—sort of. As the bartender approached, she put her quarters in the machine. He poured her a shot, and as he walked away Amy hit the coin return. She had found "heaven." She could drink for free.

The bartender commented to me that in all his days of tending bar he had not seen a person—man or woman—who could drink the way my mother does and still be standing. "I'm not. I'm sitting," Amy answered back with a chuckle.

With no sign of amusement on my face, I questioned the bartender. "Is that supposed to be a compliment?" Caught off guard, he stuttered to apologize.

But I was pleased with myself for speaking up on this occasion. What I really wanted to do was sit down and cry. I was so numb and bitter. Seeing my mother one more time was a great disappointment.

Looking at Amy through the mirror at the back of the bar, I stood motionless behind her.

Where had the years gone?

Who was this woman?

The face that haunted me—the face that scared me into calling for help that morning in the motel room—was now only a distant stranger.

I was not my mother.

I returned home the next day, leaving Amy sitting at the bar. I've not seen her since.

I wrote to my mother after returning from Vegas and explained that I needed to get on with my life, and try to let go of the past as best I can.

I have spent thirty-nine years justifying, minimizing, and discounting what my life was like. I have tried to forgive and forget the behavior of my family. But more to the point, I have spent the years justifying, minimizing, and discounting my mother. I've tried talking to her on the telephone; but she still pretends not to get it. She still professes her innocence. I've tried to tell her it is not about blame anymore. Her question lately has been, "What have I done?" It's not so easy for me to answer that question. First, I do not believe that she really gives a damn. Secondly, it is very painful for me to say or put into words what I feel about her. I remember wondering what I could do differently to get my mother to take notice of me: to like me, to hold me, to tell me I matter. I only heard "Shut up or I'll give you something to cry about," or "You think you had it so bad? Well, look what happened to me!"

Just once, it would have been nice to hear a kind word, not "After all I've done for you kids . . . "

I have to reason that she believed she was doing the best she could with what life had dealt her, but the small voice inside of me won't go away. The voice keeps asking questions: Why wasn't my mother able to love me? Why do I only remember living in fear? Why did it take my mother five years to get us out of Parmadale? Why wasn't my mother home to protect me from her drunk boyfriend?

I was so angry at her when she brought men home and then asked me to "Give uncle . . . so and so . . . a kiss!" I was so embarrassed to see her drunk.

I have tried to add up the years I lived under the same roof with her. I lived with her on and off until I was seven—then time out for living with Grandma Cicero, Uncle Guido, and not to mention the chain of babysitters and her side of the family—all before being placed in an orphanage so that my parents could continue to drink! The next and last time I lived with her was when I was twelve years old—for one year. So let's say eight years out of thirty-nine years. Why do we keep up this pretense of family? Over the years I have tried to have a relationship with her. Yet each time we see each other, or speak to each other, she has been drinking! It's not good enough that I have come across country to see her! Instead, she attacks me and want to know why I didn't stay with her or why I didn't come to her house first. When I called her in Cleveland for Mother's Day, she wanted to know why I didn't call sooner. It was eight o'clock in the morning in L.A.

When I told her about the sexual abuse I went through with Dad, her only comment was, "Well, look what he did to me!" Last year for my birthday she called, saying she wanted to send me a little some-thing.—she had helped the boys out from time to time, and that she wanted to give me some money, a thousand dollars. She asked me not to tell anyone. Later, she called me and accused me of telling my brothers. Again, it proves how little she thinks of me and how little she knows me. I didn't accept the money because I needed the money, nor did I ask for it. I accepted the money because I thought it would mean something TO HER. I thought it was possibly her way of saying she did care about me. Now I know the truth; she got the money from Lenny before he died! I know what it is to be an alco-holic woman. I know what it is to live in fear—fear of waking up in the morning, and fear of not waking. I have lost a lot over the years because of my drinking. I hated myself and everyone around me. I have worked damned hard over the past years to pull my life together. She shouldn't dare tell me again with the, "YEAH BUT"—that she had it so tough in your life. Who in this family had it easy? Life is too short. Angelo is gone. She was married to him for less than seven years—over thirty years ago. She has been remarried for twenty-five years and still refers to "what your father did to me." Drop the rock. Give it up. It's not working anymore. I do not feel sorry for her. I do not hate her. I cannot hide from my feelings anymore. I cannot live in guilt, thinking WHY? DOES MY MOTHER EVER TRY TO UNDERSTAND ME? Guilt is not a reason to keep people in our lives. I will spend the rest of my life with the people who care about me—people who love me and ask how I am doing. I have a life and family here in California. This is my home. I have lived here almost twenty years. We have only seen each other five or six DAYS in all that time. I won't/can't pretend anymore. I wish her well for the rest of her life, but I can no longer have any contact with her until she finds her sober voice.

Chapter Nineteen—The Next Generation

THE INCEST, ALCOHOL, DRUG ABUSE, VERBAL AND PHYSICAL ABUSE continues in the family. In my experience, incest isn't taboo—the taboo is talking about it! Two nieces have come forward, admitting they too had been sexually abused—one by her father, the other by an uncle. One other female cousin has admitted incest by her father. Two male second cousins, in their early twenties, have admitted to sexual abuse. How many others?

After years of not knowing what had happened to the daughter Albert walked away from, I wanted to meet with my niece. Albert finally called in 1992 with his daughter's phone number. I hadn't seen her since she was two years old, and she bitterly told me of the sexual abuse she suffered from an uncle. I didn't want to begin our relationship over the phone. How could I? How could anyone?

Returning to Cleveland this time was my decision. There were no deaths, and no dramas. I was at a point where I knew the only way to put closure on the past was to face it.

After twenty years of living in Southern California, I convinced myself that February in Ohio could not be that bad. Well, I was wrong. During my seven-day stay, the temperature high was eighteen degrees. Most people in Cleveland seemed to shrug off or live in denial about more than just the weather conditions. Only a few times would someone admit to me that this was the worst winter they had seen in several years. Usually, they said it with a smirk as they watched me trying to control my teeth from chattering.

The lifestyle is understandably slower. Just getting dressed to venture out into freezing temperatures was tiring. Driving with little visibility in a rental car proved to be challenging.

The few family members I remained in contact with seemed confused by my sudden appearance after all these years. "Have you seen your mother or brothers?" was the big question of the week. When I replied "No!" the look of surprise on the faces showed me their disapproval. It was necessary to distance myself from too much contact with anyone. I didn't come all this way to visit with old friends. I needed to focus my attention on the memories, signals, and details coming at me—knowing this would be my last trip to Cleveland.

I was on the road, waiting to make a left turn into the orphanage. I tried not to focus on the lettering etched on the surface of the huge stonewall—PARMADALE. A cold chill ran through me as I entered through the gates. Talking out loud, I needed to assure myself that I was no longer a child or a victim—that I could turn around and drive out at any time.

The road leading back inside was just as mysterious as it had been thirty-three years ago. Turning the car's engine off, I sat there for a moment and stared ahead at the cottage in front of me marked "Office," remembering the day Angelo left us there.

Slowly getting out of the car, I braced myself as I stood up on the icy sidewalk and pulled the fur collar tighter around my neck, shielding me from the severe cold. Every movement seemed endless. My knees stiffened and my voice weakened as I approached the receptionist's desk and asked to speak to anyone who might be able to give me information about the early sixties.

The woman greeted me politely, until I expressed why I was there: "I lived here." Her expression changed to an unspoken "go away" as she picked up the telephone and called someone else, explaining that "There's a woman here who claims to have lived here years ago. And she wants to see someone in records."

This was not exactly whom I had asked to see, but I knew it was a place to start. From her mannerisms, I knew it was as far as I was going to get with her. She gave me instructions on how to get to the records building. It was the cafeteria when I lived there.

A woman in her late twenties met me outside the building. After the phone call from the front office, she took advantage of the opportunity for a smoke break and stood outside in fifteen-degree weather waiting for me. As I approached, she snapped at me, "What is it that you want?"

I was not about to have traveled over twenty-eight hundred miles to be brushed off by her, yet I held my tongue to keep from blasting her. I remained calm and direct. "If you don't want to help me, I am sure I can find someone inside who will. Also, I do not intend to stand outside and discuss this matter with you."

I walked past her and into the building. She followed immediately behind me, stopping me at the desk just inside the door.

"I will need for you to fill out some forms before I can talk to you," she said.

"Fine, give me the papers!" I snapped back at her.

"I can't give you any information on anyone but yourself," she added.

"I didn't ask you for any."

She seemed bent on trying to frustrate me into leaving. "It was a long time ago. Let me see what records, if anything, are left in your file."

"I will be the judge of that when I see it," I responded.

The dance continued a few more times. She informed me it would take two or three weeks to get the information to me. She showed no sign of human kindness.

After one more failed attempt to let this rude person know that I was not the enemy—that my intentions for being there were strictly for personal knowledge and to obtain any medical records or information as to my arrival and departure dates—I informed her I was not leaving until I got the information I came for.

I also asked to see someone who could walk me through Cottage Thirteen. She looked me in the eyes and lied, telling me that it was not in use—that no one would be over there as it was used only for storage of old records. I knew this was a lie, having just driven past the cottage on my way to see her and seeing people inside through the windows.

Having enough experience in life not to let her get to me, I signed all her paperwork, thanked her, and left. I walked back outside, welcoming the coldness of the chilled air. It was warm in comparison to her hostility.

Three years of living in confinement all came back. It was not my imagination. The place still reeked of hostility and resentment. I had been carrying the rage and anger for the militant nuns.

I started toward my car. The thought of defeat or giving up at this moment did not appeal to me. I refused to give up now—something inside gave me the strength to keep going. What is she going to do—call the police and have me arrested for walking on the property?

Proceeding to walk, I crossed the parking lot toward Cottage Thirteen.

The snow covered the walkway, and it was several feet deep. I stayed on the road and followed it around to the back door. Pausing for a moment and looking out at the now bare trees of winter, I remembered how terrified I was when I ran out into the night as a child.

Now, I could see that if I had kept running—the forest was not a forest. It was only a thicket and would have led me to the main street, less than a few hundred feet away.

I walked up the stairs to the door. When I knocked on the door, a wave of emotions hit me—back was all the terror of standing out there, begging for the nun to let me in.

I waited a moment longer and then looked through the glass panel and was relieved that no one was bothering to respond to my knocking. I am sure the woman in records phoned ahead to alert them to my presence. It did not matter. The reason I was there was clear enough to me. I was finally able to release the pain of my childhood and took full advantage of standing there.

It was over. And I could walk away, sighing relief. Everything seemed to brighten. The cottage was not so enormous. The door that was locked so many years ago—the door to my heart—had finally been unlocked.

Starting back to my car, I felt a lightness I had not known. I also knew that the trip here was more than a series of coincidences or chance. I suddenly realized the two women I encountered were merely a test for me to gain back my energy or the strength I lost so many years ago. The test was for me to learn not to be so easily swayed from what my instincts tell me, that someone telling me "no" doesn't have to mean "No!"

I was free.

I noticed lightness in my step as I walked back to the car. I thanked God for carrying me through all the trials and self-doubt of my life. I asked God to forgive my arrogance, ignorance and fear of prayer all these years. I had a deep awareness of a power greater than myself.

As if from nowhere, I looked up and straight into the eyes of a woman approaching me. Joyfully, I smiled at the stranger.

She smiled back and asked if she could help me. What a contrast to the two I had encountered earlier! Silently thanking God, I responded:

"Well yes, and thank you for asking."

From that moment on, doors seemed to open. I briefly explained my reason for being there, as I had tried to explain earlier to the rude woman in records. I was interested in trying to put closure on my past. She responded kindly and said she would see what she could find for me. She then introduced herself, "Hi, I am Sister . . . "

The nun surprised me by her casual dress. I would have guessed her to be just an office clerk. She was very kind and helpful, pulling out old brochures on Parmadale's early beginnings and explaining to me that the particular order of nuns who ran the orphanage back in the sixties were no longer there. She suggested I could go out to the retirement home and talk with a Sister Ruth whom she believed was the last of the nuns from that time period. And she gave me the address.

I also asked her if I could possibly see the inside of the cottage where I had lived. I wanted to see the dorms, the white porcelain sinks lined up in a row, the shower stalls, and the lockers. Maybe this was all crazy to them, but I had come this far and wanted to see it.

But she informed me that it no longer looked as it did then. Parmadale had remodeled the insides of the cottages to accommodate the residential alcoholic and drug programs they now housed.

"What about the chapel?" I questioned.

The sister made a telephone call and informed someone that I was in her office and on my way over to see the chapel, "Could you please open the chapel for her?"

Once there, I was left alone in the chapel with instructions to let the sister know when I was leaving so she could re-lock the doors.

The room was still and empty. All the large, imposing, life-sized religious statues had been removed. The wooden church pews were replaced with chairs. I felt only sadness sitting in the room. I closed my eyes and remembered all the days I sat, knelt, and got sick there. And now, this too was over!

Before I left, I received the admissions and medical records I had requested.

I could move on now, another brick removed. Driving out, I knew I was leaving behind all the negative energy I had carried for all those years.

As I was to pass through the huge stone wall exit, I gasped at the sight of a sign on a building to my right—the sign for Holy Cross Cancer Home.

Ironically, this is where my father had lived the last few months of his life; he had died on the grounds of Parmadale.

One more stop out to the retirement home—I was too excited and drained to go that day and planned to go the first thing in the morning. Facing my fears has always been extremely difficult, but I have learned to face them anyway.

The next day I drove out to see her. Like many nuns, she too, had given up the "penguin" outfits. Sister Ruth was dressed in worn, drab attire of a below-the-knee wool skirt and a cotton blouse, covered by a loose fitting sweater that veiled her rounded body. The wooden rosary beads that used to hang down the side of their robes had been replaced by much smaller necklace-type beads. She marched in, eyeing me up and down before pointing for me to follow her into a side room. She sat down, crossing her feet and clasping her hands together on her lap. The long moment of silence was broken when she began making small talk. She informed me that all of the order of nuns that worked in Parmadale in the sixties had retired, died, or left the church. I felt no comfort in knowing this.

Without facial expression, she continued on, avoiding direct eye contact. She was the only one left here at this facility from Parmadale. Without any noticeable change in her voice or body language she stated, "It looks as if you have done quite well for yourself, Sandra. You must just put the past behind you!" With that she sat still, hands folded on her lap. She stopped talking and stared blankly at me with no eye contact.

Fighting back the lump in my throat, the tightness in my stomach, and the tears in my eyes, I tried to divert her defensiveness by explaining how much of my life had been blocked—and that I was trying to put the past behind me. But I needed to have questions answered in order to do that!

With that she informed me, "You children were very difficult to deal with."

I wanted to scream—DIFFICULT! What did you expect from children who had been torn apart by their parents and sent to live with the hostile attitudes of the self-righteous nuns? But I sat there and let the tears roll down my face, controlling the rage I felt for her smugness.

With all the sensitivity and the movement of a snail, she finally got up to get me a tissue—but only after I requested it. I took several deep breaths while she was gone, letting out a sigh and quieting my emotions in preparation for the next confrontation. It felt good to ask her to get me something, even if it was only a tissue.

Somehow, she and other people I have encountered want to believe that it was best for us to be there rather than with our parents or other family members—not an easy notion for a small child to understand. From my experience with the nuns and the systems imposed, much damage was done to my spirit, stripping trust and dignity for years.

Sister Ruth returned to the sterile surroundings of the room, positioning her body facing away from me. She commented about "how difficult it was working in Parmadale."

I looked at her in disbelief. Did she want me to feel sorry for her, for the nuns?

Sitting alone in my car before starting the engine, it occurred to me, perhaps being placed in Parmadale had saved us from even worse conditions? I let the tears come that I had been holding down. I damned the teachings of a punishing God—releasing the rage inside.

As I drove away, the anger was gone and only a deep sadness remained.

I passed a car on the road with a bumper sticker that read "It's not a choice, it's a baby."

"REALLY." How many pro-life people have lived on welfare? How many have lived in orphanages or foster homes? How many have lived with hunger—not knowing where their next meal would come from? How many have been beaten by mom, dad, or other caretakers? Most of my life I would have welcomed death. I've been able to survive, but how many others are so fortunate? How many of the "unwanted" end up in jail or the prison systems? I only wish we could find a way to prevent all the unwanted children in the world.

I have read statistics showing that one in every five women has been molested or raped. One in every eight to ten men has also been abused. And 90 percent of these people are molested by a relative or friend of the family.

The climb upward has been anything but easy. I have been blessed with wonderful teachers in my life. When I finally got sick and tired of being sick and tired, when I realized that if I kept doing the same things I would get the same results, I began to let go. Rarely today do I find myself screaming at God—to let God know that enough is enough.

Another turning point was with my last employer. I thought I had found the perfect job. After two years, I allowed his actions to push me to the depths of depression. I justified and discounted the abuse by a superior in the workplace because I forgot about integrity. I didn't want to lose a position I had worked so hard to attain. It paid good money and was close to home—working in a field I enjoyed. Unfortunately, it also meant dealing with a mean-spirited, abusive personality. I used to have a high tolerance for inappropriate behavior and not confronting others—or at least not until it reached some sort of crisis proportions.

This experience forced me to face and come to terms with my past. For this I am grateful. I regained my strength and self-esteem, and realize we no longer have to accept abusive behavior from others. I am reminded of the Twenty-Seventh Psalm.

God is my light and my salvation;
whom shall I fear?
God is the strength of my life;
 of whom shall I be afraid?
When the wicked, even mine enemies
and my foes, came upon
me to eat up my flesh, they stumbled and fell.

The end . . . is not yet in sight. How many more lives are to be affected before the evil that has plagued so many is stopped once and for all? I have thirty-five first cousins. I have three nephews and eight nieces. How many of them have already suffered abuse? How many of them will survive and break free?

Opening up and telling others about the incest was difficult. Yet, the relief experienced from the secrets and pain has made relating my story worthwhile. I telephoned the two brothers who had continued to let Angelo/Dad babysit their children. They needed to know.

My regret is that I did not find my voice sooner. My niece confided that she had been abused by her father. It had never occurred to me that my silence could harm others—that the very brother who raped me would rape his own daughter sixteen years later.

In incest survivor groups, I continued to hear the same message from others: "I didn't think anyone would believe me," "I felt so ashamed. I didn't want others to know," or, "I didn't want to upset my family."

Why must we continue to suffer silently?

Who are we protecting?

If the perpetrators are not confronted or exposed, they will continue to abuse others.

Angelo was cruel and malicious. Now, twenty years after his death, lives are still paying the price of his existence. My own scars kept me from bringing children into the world.

Looking into the eyes of the next generation, I hope to reach out, removing the pain from their faces, telling them that change is possible. Believe in yourself and in a higher power—even when it seems no one cares. Don't give up before the miracle.

My message to others is: Have courage to change, reclaim your power, and use your voice—speak up. Stop living as victims. Look for positive role models who will help you improve the quality of your life.

Reading was a wonderful escape for me. It not only gave me something to do in the moment, but it planted the seeds for hopes and dreams that one day my life would be joyous.

My intent in writing this book is not to offend anyone, but rather to raise human consciousness. I do believe my story, and one day yours, has to be told. The only way we are ever going to put a stop to the problems in our lives, homes, and families is by opening up and talking about them.

People have said, "They're only children." They say, "They won't remember."

I say they do remember.

I had been gone only seven days, but I was drained and emotionally exhausted—never so happy to see a plane take off as on this morning. I was ready to go home and put the past behind me. I knew Jeff would be waiting for me when the plane landed. He is the family I have always longed for. Together we can love, laugh, or cry; and we do remember what it was like without each other. I could finally let go of the past—able to move on into forgiveness.